JUDAS
Beloved Disciple

By

The Venerable Bill Brison

JUDAS
Beloved Disciple
By
The Venerable Bill Brison

JUDAS BELOVED DISCIPLE

iUniverse books may be ordered through booksellers or by contacting:

iUniverse
1663 Liberty Drive
Bloomington, IN 47403
www.iuniverse.com
1-800-Authors (1-800-288-4677)

ISBN: 978-1-4759-9668-5 (sc)
ISBN: 978-1-4759-9669-2 (ebk)

Printed in the United States of America

iUniverse rev. date: 08/14/2013

Dedication

Critic
"a person skilled in judging the qualities or merits of some class of things,
esp. of literary or artistic work"
Critical
"discriminating, fastidious, nice, exact, decisive"

To Peggy
beloved wife
her steadfast support and encouragement has been apparent in our work on
Judas
Beloved Disciple

To Matt Melko
beloved friend

When the spirit of truth comes he will guide
you into all the truth
John 16.13

Acknowledgements

The manuscript has been read by the following, some of who were distinguished New Testament scholars; others were eminent in other fields. All of the below, in the midst of busy professional lives, have made detailed and helpful comments.

I have been encouraged and informed by their careful consideration and have taken account of their suggestions.

Dr William E. Rutherford, linguist.

Dr Edward Roche Hardy, "go to the sources".

The Rev. Canon Charles Moule, Lady Margaret Professor of Divinity at Cambridge University.

The Rt. Rev. Dr J. A. T. Robinson when he was lecturing on John at Cambridge University.

The Rev. Brevard Childs, about the time he went from teaching Old Testament at Yale University to lecturing on the New Testament at Cambridge University.

Lord Blanch when he was Archbishop of York.

The Rt. Rev. D. E. Jenkins, Bishop of Durham.

Peggy, my wife: Over the 50 years that *Judas, Beloved Disciple* has been a work in progress, she has typed, proof read, corrected and gone over every sentence in hundreds of proofs hundred of times, suggesting and criticising in the literal meaning of the term. Matt Melko has lived with this over the 50 years, receiving proofs; he showed me that to be a critic is to destroy the dross, leaving exposed what is good and true. His criticism irritated at first, but I soon learned he knew what he was talking about. He is an internationally known scholar who studied Civilizations and Peace. In a world at war and in a culture which glorifies war, we need to understand the ingredients of peace and how to achieve it. He has written many books including the following:

Peace in the Western World McFarland & Company, Inc., Publishers
The Nature of Civilization, Porter,
Sargent Publishers.

Bill Rutherford, childhood friend, who advised me to "keep your nose to the grindstone".

Bud Chutter, DDS, childhood friend, whose dental work lasted me for 30 years.

Uncle George Pierce, a staunch Lincoln Republican, who was the youngest Freshman Senator ever in the New York state legislature.

Stanly Wilber, my grandfather, who always did two things every week; went to choir practice on Thursday and sang in the church choir on Sunday.

Rev. Simons, Sunday School Superintendent at the Glen Rock URC church. Taught me at the Vacation Church School when I was 10 years old that religion could be fun

Leroy Nettleton, my father-in-law, who was put off church because the Congregationalists were not allowed to play baseball on Sundays and the Episcopalians were.

Elsie Nettleton, my mother-in-law, walked to church twice every Sunday in Lincolnshire to sing in the choir. The horses had their day of rest.

Harry Nettleton, my brother-in-law, who found an alternative word to use when I expressed dismay at his taking Our Lord's name in vain.

National Health Service for saving my life again.

Sarah O'Brien, our daughter who drew the sketches on Pages 7, 35 and 38(42); a sketch is worth 1000 words.

James Hulme, our grandson, who at age 12 drew the sketch on the title page, catching the agony of the man who betrayed his Lord and realized it.

And also The Parish of All Saints, Newton Heath, Manchester, who demonstrated that the Beloved Disciple is too important to leave to the experts.

Titus Wilson and Sons, Printers, have gone far beyond their professional duties and what they have been paid for, in patiently and skilfully going through revision after revision after revision, in visit after visit, always with good humour.

Contents

Introduction

Judas, Beloved Disciple, could have been presented as a detective story; or as a Bible study; it could have been included in a commentary on the Fourth Gospel; or as an academic study to be read by Biblical scholars specializing in the Fourth Gospel. Or, it might have been presented as fiction, in the form of a novel. Sometime, I am going to write a commentary on the Fourth Gospel. This book is all of the above but it is not fiction. It is a simple truth. Truth is rarely simple, but it can be. This simple truth has a profound lesson for each and every person. This truth affirms the place and potency of forgiveness in the wonderful treasury of all that Jesus did and taught.

It is important in reading this book to start where the author started years ago. I started with reading the four incidents where the term *Beloved Disciple* is used. I suggest that you start here, by reading the four sections. They are, in the Gospel according to St. John (henceforth referred to as the Fourth Gospel):

*John 13.21-30 The Upper Room
*John 19.25-27 The Crucifixion
*John 20.1-10 The Empty Tomb
*John 21 The Resurrection Appearance by the Seas of Tiberias

In the words of the Book of Common Prayer "read, mark, learn and inwardly digest" the accounts of these four incidents. This is your "homework" and necessary if you are going to experience the mystery and thrill of discovery. So I suggest that you not rush this process. At this point, I must ask you to show some discipline. Please don't skip ahead to find my answers until you have had a chance to come to your own conclusions.

---

* It is worth noting as we begin, that the English word, ***love***, bears a large burden in that it is used in various contexts to translate the Greek words: eros, "*sexual love*"; philia, "*social love*"; storge, "*family affection*"; philadelphia, "*love between brothers and/or sisters*"; philanthropia, *humanity, kindness, courtesy*; agapao, "*like*". The first century Christian world adopted and adapted the hitherto colourless and weak word (agapao) and imbued it with the strength of God's love for man, as expressed in Jesus' love for us, and our reciprocity of that love in all the phases of the Greek words. Thus ***agapao,*** is translated into English as the very passionate word, ***love***, the operative word in the Christian vocabulary. It will be helpful to keep this in mind as you read further.

After I had read these four incidents over and over, with the aid of many commentaries on the text, and Dean Clarence Mendell, Yale University Professor commented on my translation of the Greek words for love, with much prayer, I came to ask myself

The **Why** Question.

Do you also wonder: **WHY?**

Why is the *Beloved Disciple* there at all?

Were not all twelve *Beloved?*

A Methodology

Working Hypothesis starts with a postulate (an idea, a premise, a possible explanation) and goes on to test this against the evidence. In this study, the postulate is arrived at in The Why Question. Then we proceed to test this against the evidence, internal in the Four Gospels and external in the writings of the early church fathers; the text has also been sent to and read by eminent 20th century scholars (see Acknowledgements). In very slow stages, premise by premise, fact by fact, we move the working hypothesis forward from one of possibility to one of probability to one of **reasonable certainty**.

The Working Hypothesis Extended

The *primary source* of the Fourth Gospel is the Beloved Disciple who was an eyewitness of the events he records. John, the Disciple, one of the Twelve, served as a highly skilled and knowledgeable editor who added and incorporated his own experience into the text; this is the second stage. The next stages were done by John's own disciples, his community of followers; they contributed of their own skills, proof reading and polishing the Greek of the text. This was done under the supervision of John and the Beloved Disciple. There were no substantial changes to the text after they died. The Fourth Gospel, then, is primarily the work of the Beloved Disciple, the source, and John, the editor.

The Working Hypothesis Tested

It follows that the identity of the deliberately mysterious figure of the Beloved Disciple is of paramount importance. This is investigated in as follows. It is in the answer to *The Why Question* the mystery begins to unravel. Who Was He? This is explored and established in *The Why Question*. This investigation is the great academic and spiritual adventure of my life. The Biblical (internal) evidence for this hypothesis is examined in Chapters II, III, IV and V. The external evidence of the church fathers is given in Chapter VI.

TWO DIFFICULTIES

Before we go further, there are two difficulties to accepting the thesis of this study, best posed in two questions:

Question 1 Did Judas commit suicide after he betrayed Jesus?

Judas' death is reported in two places:

> When Judas, his betrayer, saw that he was condemned, he repented and brought back the thirty pieces of silver to the chief priests and the elders, saying, "I have sinned in betraying innocent blood." They said, "What is that to us? See to it yourself." And throwing down the pieces of silver in the temple, he departed; and he went and hanged himself. But the chief priests, taking the pieces of silver, said, "It is not lawful to put them into the treasury, since they are blood money." So they took counsel, and bought with them the potter's field, to bury strangers in. Therefore that field has been called the Field of Blood to this day. Then was fulfilled what had been spoken by the prophet Jeremiah, saying, "And they took the thirty pieces of silver, the price of him on whom a price had been set by some of the sons of Israel, and they gave them for the potter's field, as the Lord directed me."
>
> Matthew 27:3-10

> In those days Peter stood up among the brethren (the company of persons was in all about 120) and said, "Brethren, the scripture had to be fulfilled, which the Holy Spirit spoke beforehand by the mouth of David, concerning Judas who was guide to those who arrested Jesus. For he was numbered among us, and was allotted his share in this ministry. (Now this man bought a field with the reward of his wickedness; and falling headlong he burst open in the middle and all his bowels gushed out. And it became known to all the inhabitants of Jerusalem, so that the field was called in their language Akeldama, that is, Field of Blood). For it is written in the Book of Psalms, 'Let his habitation become desolate, and let there be no one to live in it,' and 'His office let another take.'"
>
> Acts 1:15-20

These two accounts differ in how Judas' death occurred. In one (Matthew), Judas hanged himself; in the other (Acts) "he burst open in the middle and all his bowels gushed out."

These two accounts are irreconcilable except with an ingenuity pressing the limits of credibility. He could have found a tree in a field (by definition a cleared area), climbed it, hung himself and the effort of the struggle resulted in a massive rupture. If he had done this, hanging from the tree with a noose around his neck, he would not have fallen unless the tree branch broke.

These two accounts agree on one curious detail; that there was a field purchased with the money of betrayal and this was called the Field of Blood, Akeldama. However, in Matthew, it was the chief priests who purchased the field (Matthew 27:6-7). In Acts, it was Judas who purchased the field (Acts 1:18)

Further, we note that Mark doesn't mention Judas' suicide; nor do Luke or John, although Luke and Acts are by the same author. In most detail, Matthew and Luke follow Mark. It is interesting that in Matthew's account, the chief priests would seem to be the source of the account of the suicide. Matthew is the most Jewish of the gospels. Whilst in Luke/Acts, the source must have been the early Christian community. Each of these two communities, Jewish and Christian, had compelling reasons to make a scapegoat of Judas. The Jewish community needed to disguise their disreputable role in the crucifixion. The Jews said, "We have no King but Caesar" (John 19:15). Jews for two thousand years before and two thousand years after the crucifixion acknowledged *only* the kingship of God.

Answer to Question 1
The two versions or traditions of Judas' death are irreconcilable: logic has it that one must be wrong – which?; or, as one Biblical scholar commented, "the likelihood is that both are wrong". Nonetheless, when we challenge the veracity of Bible tradition, we must be prepared to give reasons why. It is evident that the first century Jewish and Christian communities had ample reason to make a scapegoat of Judas. Several decades intervened between the time of the crucifixion and the appearance of Matthew's and Luke's gospels. The fact that Mark didn't record the death indicates that Matthew and Luke/Acts much later uncovered the stories of Judas' suicide. Subsequent generations, including our own, find in Judas a convenient excuse for our own guilt, for the guilt of all humankind, for the crucifixion of Jesus. Certainly Judas was guilty of a heinous crime and he has given his very name to the act of betrayal. It is my contention that this widespread and communal (Jewish and Christian) *death wish* gave birth to the *rumours* of Judas' suicide. Or, as Shakespeare put it, "The wish was father to the thought." In conclusion, we might note that Bishop Irenaeus, writing in the second century, commented on The Judas Gospel, calling it "fictitious history". What he didn't say was that Judas couldn't possibly have produced a gospel because he committed suicide after the crucifixion. There were other traditions that Judas had not died shortly after the crucifixion. There was an early sect, the followers of Judas, who were said to worship the devil.

Was there a kernel of truth here (that Judas lived on)?

Question 2
Could Judas *possibly* have been forgiven?
There is ample evidence in Jesus' words and actions that Judas was forgiven, before as well as after, the act of betrayal. Judas was included in the band of Twelve at the Last Supper when Jesus offered them his body and his blood. Judas was likewise present when Jesus washed the disciples' feet. Jesus did not identify Judas as the betrayer when he had the opportunity. As he hung on the cross, Jesus gave his mother into the hands of the Beloved Disciple when he said, "Woman, behold, your son". In John 21:20 Jesus refused to *pass sentence* on the Beloved Disciple. Judas was forgiven by Jesus. Can we forgive Judas? Can we do without our scapegoat? For we, too, are guilty of betraying Jesus (like Judas), denying him (like Peter), fading into the background (like the other disciples). To give up Judas means we have to face our guilt.

Answer to Question 2
The scope of God's forgiveness is perhaps best expressed in the poetry of three hymns

> Amazing Grace
> How sweet the sound
> That saved a wretch like me
> I once was lost
> But now am found
> Was blind but now I see
> *John Newton 1723-1807*

> Could Judas be forgiven?
> Is *grace* anything less than *amazing*?
> Can we put limits on God's mercy?

In the words of another familiar hymn:
> There's a wideness in God's mercy like the wideness of the sea
> There's a kindness in his justice which is more than liberty
> There is welcome for the sinner and more graces for the good
> There is mercy with the Saviour, there is healing in his blood

> There is no place where earth's sorrows are more felt than up in heaven
> There is no place where earth's failures have such kindly judgment given
> There is plentiful redemption in the blood that has been shed

There is joy for all the members in the sorrows of the Head
Frederick William Faber 1814-1863
We can add the words of another hymn (that Judas was):
"Ransomed, healed, restored forgiven"
Henry Francis Lyte (1793-1847)

To conclude, Professor Charles Moule wrote:
"I am deeply touched by your beautiful thought about Our Lord's forgiveness of Judas" . . . "and about the Christian community's forgiveness of him?"

(Author's comment: Charles wasn't certain about the Christian community, nor am I).

Now you are ready to go on to my answer to the WHY Question. This answers leads to another Question:
The WHO Question

The Why Question

A question that has intrigued readers of the Fourth Gospel from the beginning has been the question of *who* the mysterious figure, "the disciple whom Jesus loved", could be. The question of authorship is closely related. Guesses have been made and are still being made. But the underlying question, surely, is the *why* question. This question, too, is intriguing, and the answer to it might provide the answer to the *who* question. What is the *why* question?

The question is: Why did the author (or authors, or editors or redactors or a combination thereof) who otherwise seems a sensible person, choose what appears to be a nonsensical circumlocution by designating one of the twelve disciples in a way which is used by no other Evangelist, was unknown by the early Church, apparently unknown by the twelve disciples and probably even to Jesus himself, and then substitute this designation for the commonly known name of one of the Twelve at key points in the narrative?

Some answers have been given. Bultmann thinks that the author invented this figure to symbolize Gentile Christianity, as St. Mary the Virgin symbolized Jewish Christianity. But most commentators find it hard to believe that the author would invent such a character, put words in his mouth, and write him into such important scenes in the Gospel.

It may be that the "Beloved Disciple" figure is accidental or capricious or a fluke of some kind. But I believe there is a pattern, a purpose with a strong motivation, pursued by a very shrewd and determined disciple and theologian.

The "Beloved Disciple" may be mysterious. He is not nebulous, he is not at all wraithe-like, he is not depersonalized, as one would expect a symbol to be. In the incidents in which he appears he plays an important and individualized part. He enters into significant dialogue with Jesus. He is a key figure in such important places as the Upper Room, at the foot of the Cross, at the Empty Tomb and in the resurrection appearance at the Sea of Tiberias. It is hard to believe he was invented for symbolic, or other, reasons.

There aren't many other answers to the *why* question. Goulder in a lecture on the authorship of the Fourth Gospel has said that concealment of authorship was necessary, and he works into this theory that the author was Nathaniel, one of the twelve become Dositheus, an early Christian Gnostic heretic. This is a cogent attempt to answer the *Why* question, although this answer to who the Beloved Disciple was is highly speculative. Vernard Eller, writing in 1987, puts a case for the Beloved Disciple being Lazarus, even more highly speculative. Other scholars believe that the Fourth Gospel has undergone so many redactions or stages as to make the question of *why* the "Beloved Disciple" so obscure as to largely make it irrelevent and unanswerable.

However, it is the assumption of this study that the Fourth Gospel is largely the product of, and has as its primary source, a single mind, that this person was a disciple and an eyewitness of most of what he writes about, that he was a shrewd and perceptive observer, that he was a scrupulous and careful historian, as well as being a man of deep faith and a brilliant theologian. Furthermore, by nature and because of his theological position (e.g. "the word became flesh and dwelt among us") he was particularly concerned to be accurate in the reporting of the events of Jesus' ministry on earth. The fact that a knowledge of what happened was not in itself adequate to understanding Jesus, that the events were "signs", should not obscure the author's belief that these "signs" were rooted in historical events. It follows that if he used the circumlocution of the "Beloved Disciple" he did so deliberately, intelligently and for an important reason.

The statement above about the author covers a lot of critical ground. Suffice it to say that there is a respectable body of critical opinion which would support that kind of statement. Bishop Westcott, in the 19th century, gave potent, and to my mind valid, reasons in that direction. John A. T. Robinson, 50 years ago diffidently in *Twelve New Testament Studies*[1], and more thoroughly in *Redating the New Testament*[2] has advanced arguments which make such an assumption about the author reasonable. This short study then shelters under the wing of scholars Westcott and Robinson.

Martin Hengel in *The Johannine Question* argues, with an impressive and almost encyclopedic knowledge and, to my mind conclusively, that "Furthermore, it seems to me unmistakable that the Gospel and the letters are not the expression of a community with many voices, but above all the voice of a **towering theologian**, the founder and head of the Johannine school".[3]

As for my own answer to the *why* question, it was some years ago, while puzzling about the events in the Upper Room, that a crazy idea came to me. It

---

[1] Robinson, J. A. T., *Twelve New Testament Studies*, article "The New Look on the Fourth Gospel", page 94ff.

[2] Robinson, J. A. T., *Redating the New Testament*, page 308-12.

[3] Hengel, Martin, *The Johannine Question*, page IV.

was quickly tossed out as being preposterous. But it refused to remain submerged. In the reading and lecturing I did on the Fourth Gospel from then on it kept recurring. Each time it was with the feeling that it was a little less preposterous; it was not so easily disproved, and it intrigued me more and more. In the past years I have had time to investigate this more fully, and I found the idea not only was not invalidated but received substance and credibility. The further I went, the more I read what others had written, the more I tested the hypothesis, the more the pieces fell into place and the more I became convinced.

This crazy idea is that the disciple Judas Iscariot, the one who betrayed Jesus, was the "Beloved Disciple", also the author of the Fourth Gospel. The answer to the why question is that the term, "Beloved Disciple", was used deliberately and because of the absolute necessity of hiding the identity (as Goulder) of the real author, i.e. Judas. Thus the "Beloved Disciple" is a necessary device (clever and anonymous, a cipher) to separate Judas from authorship. Even after (or especially after) several decades, the prejudice about Judas was firmly established and deeply engrained in the Christian and Jewish communities. The need to hide the authorship was that Judas (and his close associates?) was afraid, and justly so, that if it were generally known that he were the source, the author, his Gospel, which he rightly regarded as being of inestimable value to the church, would be thoroughly discredited and perhaps completely lost. This is the basic theory of this study. I don't expect that many will believe it at this stage. I do hope that the reader will not discard the idea out of hand as ridiculous but will read the following chapters. The theory doesn't rest upon any one word, text, incident or interpretation, but on the preponderance of evidence, so please look at the evidence. The case, by its nature, cannot be proved, but the bulk of evidence, the preponderance of evidence, makes the thesis not only possible but probable. It can be tested at any of a number of different points against the Biblical evidence and not shown defective or even improbable.

The primary evidence for the authorship of the Fourth Gospel is and has to be by its very nature in the Fourth Gospel itself (where else?). It follows that the detailed answer to the Why Question is in the Fourth Gospel itself and, more particularly, in the use of the term, *Beloved Disciple*, and the places where this designation is used. The key to understanding why it is used is to examine in detail the places it is used. This is the content of **Chapter II**. In **Chapters III, IV** and **V**, we examine other internal evidence. The external evidence of the early church fathers is given in **Chapter VI**. In so far as practicable the major texts themselves are given. In each chapter the Working Hypothesis is tested against the evidence.

The analysis in the preceeding paragraph has passed over **Chapters I** and **II**. This is for two very different reasons. **Chapter I**, distills in a conjectural mode, the life of Judas based upon evidence of the other chapters. Although it is conjecture and assumption, it is conjecture and assumption based upon what we know about the life, times and teaching of Jesus; what we know about Judas; and our knowledge of the early church. It is placed before the other chapters because it is a distillation of their evidence.

Chapter VIII describes the astounding and very welcome news in National Geographic of the discovery of the long lost *The Judas Gospel*. This news is astounding because this document has been lost for 1800 years and found in a bank vault in Hicksville, New York, of all places. It is welcome news because it looks very much like an early effort that Judas might have floated to see what would happen. Judas has always been newsworthy. He is prominent in productions like *Jesus Christ Superstar* and *Godspell*, and has a fascination all his own, the fascination of evil.

This study could have been presented, as a novel, as a study in the nature of evil, of sin and forgiveness, as an ecclesiastical detective story or as a legal brief. I have chosen to present it as a Biblical study because, in the final analysis, that is where the evidence is and where the judgement on its veracity must be made. In any case, I hope that the reader will experience some of the thrill of discovery, and the awe at the sense of the scope of Christ's forgiveness and reconciling power, which I have felt as I have worked this out.

The Answer to the WHY Question
"The Beloved Disciple" knew he had to disguise his true identity to ensure that the Fourth Gospel would get "published" and get a fair hearing. He chose a very clever "disguise". There were Twelve "Beloved Disciples"; only one of the Twelve was where he was, saw what he saw, heard what he heard and did what he did.

The Who Question follows
WHO WAS HE?
Incredible as it is, the only credible answer is:
JUDAS

This is not entirely an original idea; as perceptive a scholar as William Barclay speculated that this might be the case.

Chapter I

I, JUDAS
My Life
Reconstructed

Based on what we know of life in Palestine in the first century, of our knowledge of the life and teaching of Jesus; what we know about Judas; our knowledge of the early church and its Jewish origins; and in the writings of the early church fathers; but mainly on the New Testament sources and 'predominately on the Fourth Gospel'.*

A. **The Story**

What follows is an imaginative reconstruction of the life of Judas written in the first person.

I, Judas Iscariot, son of Simon Iscariot, am a man from Kerioth, that is, from the town of Kerioth in Judea, the only Judean among the Twelve Apostles. As such I don't have the ties that unite the rest of the apostolic band, most of whom were Galilean fishermen, and some of whom are related. Nonetheless I acquired an important position among the twelve. I was a particular friend of Peter and, with Peter, at the centre of the apostolic band. I am only being honest when I say that I am intelligent, sensitive and a careful observer. Although I was an outsider, Jesus made me treasurer, the only office The Twelve had. The job wasn't easy. Jesus trusted me. The money was completely my responsibility. No one else knew who gave us money and for what reason and how it was spent. I wore a leather coat with large pockets enabling me to keep the *accounts separate*. There was no yearly audit, not even a probing question. Unfortunately, I got in the habit of dipping my hand into the *till*. At first it was nothing really serious, only a copper or two. Money can be seductive. Money is important. Jesus spoke about money often; he knew a lot about it and how

---

* Robert Graves, a distinguished scholar, adopted a similar approach in his widely acclaimed book, *I, Claudius* (also a TV series).

1

important it is. I felt a pang each time he mentioned money. Did he know about my little *borrowings*? I didn't think so at the time but in retrospect when he knew that I was to betray him, I'm not so sure. In any case, I went from the bad habit of borrowing joint funds, fully intending to pay back, to a *loan* larger than can be repaid, to a permanent loan which was, in effect, and to my astonishment, stealing. I knew other people who did this. I justified this in various ways. In practice there is a fine line between money used for the common good and money used for my own good. After all, I was a disciple, what benefited me, benefited the apostolic band. The fact was that they didn't know, and I didn't want them to know. I later came to regard this petty stealing as the beginning of my moral deterioration. The little deceptions about money received and expenditures was the slippery slope that drew me into stealing (there is no other word for it). Jesus had high expectations of me, and I of him. I loved the Lord deeply, as was my nature, I knew that Jesus loved me. I believed in him; I had high expectations for him.

Then I began to have doubts. I could accept the Jesus who was Rabbi, the greatest teacher we had ever heard. I could accept the Jesus who had welded the twelve disparate men into one band, a unique and glorious fellowship such as we, and the world, had never known. I could accept the Lord who healed, the Lord who spoke to women on an equal basis with men, the Lord who in a wonderful manifestation of the outpouring of love, fed 5,000 out of practically nothing. But then Jesus began to talk, and he talked and he talked and he made all kinds of extravagant claims. He said, "I am the bread of life". He even compared himself to Moses to the detriment, apparently, of Moses.

He claimed a unique relationship with God. I had more doubts. I couldn't bring myself to voice these doubts. Men like Peter and Thomas, blunt and impulsive, just said it, blurted it out. I couldn't. It was not my nature. I tended to be reserved, to keep quiet until I had thought things out thoroughly before I made a statement or asked a question. By that time the opportunity often had passed.

My doubts were too basic, too close to what the Pharisees were saying, and I didn't want to be tarred with their brush. The basic problem, I thought later, was concerned with love and trust. I loved the Lord too much to want to hurt him, and I didn't trust him enough to share my doubts. I didn't fully appreciate how capably Jesus could deal with doubt, excuse making and downright opposition even from the faithful Twelve. If I had, if I had had the courage and humility to speak out, things might have been different. But that is the way I am, I thought later, and I've got to live with the way I am and what I have done.

Almost as bad as my doubts were the feeling that Jesus knew about them, and that he might even know about the stealing. He was so adept at reading body language and facial expressions that he sometimes seemed to know what was in our very minds. This feeling became a certainty after the feeding of the 5,000. For Jesus said to The Twelve when others of his followers dropped away: "Did I not choose you, the twelve, and one of you has a devil?" I knew then, of whom he was speaking. I had this devil – doubt, this evil inside, eating, gnawing away at my soul, my most secret and fiercely held beliefs.

I didn't know at that time the extent of Jesus' knowledge, that Jesus thought I was going to betray him. If I had known, I would have done away with myself at that moment. Or, would I? Would it have turned out any different? Could I have resisted that devil inside? (Would not Jesus still have died on the Cross?)

As time went by, I found myself listening, more and more, to the arguments of the Pharisees. Jesus described them as "hypocrites", whitened sepulchers. This was a harsh judgment. I began to see that the Pharisees had something. God is God and man is man. It is the worst kind of egotism to refer to oneself as the Son of God. Worse, it is blasphemy.

There was no way around it. The Lord I love is going in the wrong direction. He says, "I am the good shepherd". "I am the resurrection and the life". How could Jesus say these things? If he would just restrain himself, stick to the essentials, healing people, teaching, enjoying life a little more, relaxing and not going out of his way to antagonize the authorities, who, after all, had immense responsibilities to protect the people from religious fanatics and quacks whilst at the same time trying to keep the Romans happy, then everyone would calm down. The Pharisees, after all, meant well, and the Sanhedrin had its role to play.

But Jesus didn't keep quiet, and I couldn't find the words to warn him of what was coming. As time went by it began to affect my feeling for Jesus. I no longer loved him with that single minded adulation, that unrestrained enthusiasm, that simple acceptance. I tried (God knows how I tried), to rekindle the old love. For a while it would work, and then Jesus would make some further grandiose claim, and it would disappear. It boiled over in a trivial incident. Mary was being stupid and emotional again. They were having supper. Martha, as usual, was doing the work. Mary was sitting around trying to join in the conversation and then that silly girl suddenly and impulsively took the ointment, some of which I had bought her and given to her secretly. She poured it all over Jesus' feet – all of it, every last drop. The place reeked of the stuff. And Jesus just sat there with a look of infinite tenderness on his face. It wasn't that I really felt that way about the poor, but I thought Jesus would, or should. So for the first time in my life, that discipline, or reserve, or whatever, snapped; and I blurted out a protest. It was the wrong reason, the wrong occasion. Much later, analysing my feelings, I felt that I might simply have been jealous of Jesus' love for Mary. Or maybe I was jealous of Mary's love for Jesus, giving Jesus the gift I had meant for her. Who knows? Later, I wondered why I hadn't made my protest in my usual reasoned, intelligent manner, not protesting over some little thing that Mary had done. I certainly had a point about the poor. Here I thought I was an intelligent, rational human being, if anything a little above the rest of the disciples; or, let's face it, I thought that intellectually I was a good deal above them. I thought this, but at this important crisis in my life I acted like a nincompoop. It was the fault of that devil inside me again. But these were reflections I made much later when I had plenty of time. And so my hatred simmered inside me. The more I had loved, the higher my expectations had been, the lower I fell. At times I knew I was falling. I felt life slipping away. But I felt I could do nothing about it. And the notion grew within me that I must do something about Jesus, do something or go completely mad. Jesus was becoming a dangerous fanatic. Before Jesus was finished, we would be involved in a bloody war, Jew against Jew, and the Romans against us all.

The Pharisees and high priests were right. The Romans wouldn't let this go on forever. It was better that one man die for everyone than to have an insurrection, just because of the extravagant claims of one man. The procession into Jerusalem proved the point. The people hailed him as Messiah. Before then the excuse could be made that he hadn't trumpeted his claims, those who came could listen, but the rest could stay away and think what they might. The Romans might have been persuaded to deal with him as simply some kind of religious fanatic. But here he was, brazenly going into Jerusalem hailed as Messiah and King. It was public now, no doubt about it. Something must be done! I had broad shoulders, I would act as a lightning rod. There didn't seem to be anyone else in the apostolic band who would take the initiative, so the responsibility fell to me. As first I felt like a traitor, but I kept telling myself that it was a job that had to be done and a courageous man was needed to do it. Jesus must be stopped, for his own good, for the good of his apostles (who would probably all end up murdered otherwise), for the good of society, for the good of Israel, and for God's sake. His name must not be sullied any longer.

So I bided my time. After (Palm) Sunday Jesus became suddenly, and uncharacteristically, cautious. Jesus had decided, of his own free will and against our advice, to come to Jerusalem. He had entered the city boldly, he taught in public during the daytime – not only in public, but in the Temple itself! Why couldn't he show a little common sense? Why couldn't he have been less confrontational? The Pharisees were furious. But they were afraid to try to arrest him during the daytime because he had wide support among the people. It might have caused a riot and this was the last thing we wanted. At night, when they could have seized him quietly, and without any fuss Jesus went out of the city. Jesus was not quite so 'head in the clouds' as we thought. But we will get him. I had been in secret contact with the high priests. I knew Annas personally and had had conversations with him on theological and political matters. I considered myself a personal friend. I respected Annas and was flattered by the attention shown to me by him and by the respect with which my opinions were received. I liked being in the mainstream of Jewish religious life. Then I made the fatal contact with the high priests. This contact was made with the help of Nicodemus, who was a moderate member of the Sanhedrin. Nicodemus was attracted by Jesus' teaching but being a cautious man, thought that Jesus, too, should be cautious. He felt that Jesus should have a fair trial and the best way to defuse the whole explosive situation was for Jesus to be arrested secretly, given a fair hearing, probably receive a caution, and, if he agreed to modify his teaching, be allowed to continue. It was suggested that the Passover might be the time for the arrest. The populace would be busy with the Passover and unlikely to cause problems. Jesus would certainly eat the Passover with his disciples, probably at an evening meal in the city – that would be the time! And it was, but even here Jesus outwitted us. First of all, he did the Passover a day early (typically sloppy about details, why couldn't he even do that right?) And then, instead of just announcing in a straightforward way that we were going to eat the Passover at such and such a place, Jesus very cleverly concealed his intention. I didn't find this out until later. But Jesus had actually arranged for a room secretly and well ahead. Further, he had arranged to have a follower carrying a pitcher of water, unknown to any of the disciples, to meet two of them and lead them to the room so they could get things ready. This was done, not to avoid or delay arrest and death, but so he could spend uninterrupted time in the Upper Room with his Twelve Disciples and thus undisturbed celebrate with them a last supper, a rite built on the Passover and which became his gift to the Church, the sacramental remembrance of his ministry and of his self offering. I hadn't known when or where the Passover was being held until I got there with the rest. This secrecy on Jesus' part added to my list of grievances. As I looked at it later, even this didn't make any sense. Jesus had, at the least the right to protect himself. But, of course, as it turned out, it wasn't, in the final analysis, self protection he wanted. It was just the certainty of eating the Passover without interruption. That isn't, however, the way I looked at it at the time. I was furious over what I alleged to be Jesus' duplicity. It was a good kind of fury; it added steel to my resolve, justification to my cause.

My anger also affected my reasoning. Because, at the Last Supper, Jesus made one last attempt. And if I hadn't been so blinded by my self-righteous indignation, I might still have made it, have resisted that devil (another if). Did God intend it this way from the beginning, or is that just an excuse?. I arrived at the Passover with the rest of them, not knowing where it was going to be until I arrived. I had agreed with the high priests to let them know what was going on. They had insisted on giving me the money, and I took it, to refuse would have seemed churlish but that wasn't the point. I **didn't** do it for the money. I didn't think of it as blood money and I could always give the money to the poor, or buy something for Mary. After all, we'd been wandering around for three years, not knowing where my next loaf was coming from. We'd given up a lot for Jesus. I see these now as more excuses; I am clear now that I did wrong, grievous wrong, a hideous wrong. God forgive me. Hindsight is always better; Jesus was crucified. The high priests had said they wouldn't hurt Jesus, just persuade him to cool the situation a while, show a little restraint, or, if he wouldn't do that, keep him under some kind of protective custody, for his own sake, they said, because someone was going to get him sooner or later. "People" (not named, they never are) were getting very upset about this business. Someone was going to take the law into his own hands. It was better that it be done decently and in order.

At the Last Supper Jesus really pulled out all the stops: He washed our feet. I thought it was ridiculous and even embarrassing at the time, but it moved me deeply nonetheless. He had me right next to him at table, at his side. He even brought up the subject of betrayal himself. I had wondered if he knew. But how could he? I had been so careful making the arrangements. Annas had promised not to let anyone know. Or could it be that maid? Anyway, Jesus brought it up, that someone was going to betray him. And then that oaf Peter did it. He asked me to ask Jesus who it was going to be. I almost panicked. What if Jesus told them? They would have believed him. I was too far into it to back out by that time. What could I do? There was only one thing to do, and I did it. Peter couldn't hear what I was saying, but he could see my lips moving. If I didn't say anything he might blurt out the question himself in his usual insensitive way. So, with my heart in my stomach, I asked Jesus. And he seemed to understand. When he answered very quietly so no one else could hear, and gave me the sop, I knew that he knew. The pathetic thing was that he knew and yet knowing, he was willing to give me his body and blood and let me go through with the betrayal and was not even going to expose me to the rest. At the time I thought it must be a kind of death wish. Or maybe he had come to agree with us that the best thing was to go quietly, not make a fuss, and when things had died down, go on healing and teaching as before. The Pharisees wouldn't have objected to that (subject to a few restraints on what he taught and who and how

The Upper Room

John 13:23-24. One of his disciples, whom Jesus loved, was lying close to the breast of Jesus. So lying thus . . . he said to him "Lord, who is it?"

he healed, of course). (Even so, even thinking this way, I nearly wavered. I felt so close to him, and I loved him so much.

The moment passed. I could feel my heart harden. There was no going back. I told myself I was just being soft; I would do it. The devil really took possession of me then. It had to be done, I would do it. In fact, Jesus said the same thing, **"Do it quickly"**. So I went out into the dark, and it was so dark. The darkness seemed to come at me, seeping into my lungs, blanking out my mind and will, filling my very soul. I had no will, I just went on, leaving the light and the warmth, the fellowship and the love behind. How could I have? But I did, and I must accept that and live with it.

I then went to the chief priests. I had a good idea of where Jesus would go after the meal; a favourite retreat spot. We set out after a suitable interval. I told them where to go, and then I stayed in the rear, out of the torchlight and out of sight, I hoped. When we got to the Garden of Gethsemane I edged round the arresting force unobtrusively, so I wouldn't be associated with the arresting force. Then I stepped forward to kiss, the signal with which we agreed I would identify Jesus. I had thought this through carefully. The kiss was the best way. I wasn't ashamed of what I was doing. After it was all over and Jesus was freed, I would be vindicated. I realised that some of the apostles were impulsive; Peter had a sword, and it wasn't impossible that Peter would forget himself and take a swipe at me. If I tried to gesture or to tell the arresting force who Jesus was I would have to be close enough to either the disciples or to the arresting force and I might have been overheard or seen. It is quite easy to identify a person being pointed at, even when the observer is not in the line of fire. No, the kiss was the right way to do it. The disciples, I had reasoned, might even congratulate me (thinker) for acting decisively and in all of their best interests. I realised it wasn't a very nice way of doing it, as far as Jesus was concerned, but Jesus knew I was the betrayer and he could do what he wanted to protect himself. When the time came for the kiss, however, I got confused. Jesus didn't need to be identified. He spoke up. I heard him as in a dream. I had resolved to identify him with the kiss. I was unable to change my tactic. I stumbled forward, clumsily, awkwardly, and then . . . I just couldn't ever remember what did happen. Matthew and Mark say that I did kiss him, and I accept that, but I couldn't remember it. It was too terrible to remember. Every time I thought about it I felt sick, so I stopped thinking about it. I could see that my fears about possible retaliation were justified when Peter drew his sword and cut off Malchus' ear (acting impulsively as always). Years later, I think that what did happen was that I stepped forward, put my hands on my Lord's shoulders, usually a preliminary to a kiss, but that I didn't actually kiss him. Not that it makes much difference, but a kiss?, a sign of affection, turned into a sign of betrayal? One more thing for Jesus to forgive.

After the arrest there was confusion among the disciples and they fled, as Jesus had said they would. That is, all fled but Peter and me, both of whom, in different ways, deserted Jesus in body, if not in spirit. Peter started after Jesus. I, his good friend, tagged along behind. I felt the beginnings of an awful regret. They had bound the Lord, in spite of the fact that he made no resistance. They needn't have done that; he was going along. There was confusion in the air, along with incipient violence. The soldiers and the high priests' men were acting like they had wished Jesus had resisted. They had been spoiling for a fight; aching to deal decisively with this strange man and his blasphemous teaching ("turn the other cheek"); how could the world cope on this basis? A fight had been denied them and they resented it. I began to see signs of that intense, irrational hatred that they bore for Jesus. And there was Jesus, in the midst of that terrible scene, in the midst of the mob, calm in the midst of confusion, dignified in the midst of indignity, loving in the midst of hate, tender and kind in the midst of violence and cruelty, rational in the midst of an irrational mob. I trailed along behind partly because I was afraid of what I had done, partly because I was curious as to what would happen, partly because I thought I might help, partly because I thought I would remind Annas of his assurance that no harm would be done to Jesus, partly because Peter was there and we had always been close and done things together, partly because of a sense of impending tragedy, partly because I couldn't think what else to do, partly (I later thought) because God was guiding me to be a witness to something very important for a special reason.

When they reached the high priest's court, I could easily gain entry. I was almost one of the family and known to the servants. I had some misgivings about letting Peter see my familiarity with the high priest's staff, but there was no avoiding it; I had to get Peter in. Peter and I were the only disciples there and I was beginning to feel lonely, very lonely, a precursor of that terrible loneliness and despair that caused me to lose my mind for a while. I witnessed Peter's denial. It made me sick, not only because of Peter's confusion and cowardice, but because it reminded me of what I had done. Because I was seeing to Peter and witnessing Peter's denials, I missed the detail of the 'trial' before the High Priest. But I was aware of the atmosphere and it wasn't right. It wasn't what I had been led to expect. They weren't merely going to take Jesus into custody for the good of the nation and the Jewish religion. Jesus had already been struck. They were trying to bait him. Things were not going as I had let myself be persuaded they would. And I began to see with an awful

9

clarity that the Pharisees' hatred had always been apparent; they hadn't even tried to conceal it. Nicodemus and I (and some of the more moderate Pharisees) had not really even allowed ourselves to be duped. We had duped and deluded ourselves; The trial was not a fair trial. Nicodemus might have tried to protest but his protest was hardly heard; it was irrelevant; minds had been closed; hearts had been hardened. I was unable as usual to say what needed to be said at the moment. I thought a lot but said nothing, taking some perverted satisfaction from the scene of Peter's humiliation. The moderates were not being heard and were totally ineffective. The mob (no less a mob because they were the highest court of the land) were conducting a kangaroo court. I was absolutely appalled. I had no idea it was going to go this way. Rational men, men I knew and respected as pillars of religion, were behaving like a lynch mob. I saw with an awful clarity, my own naïveté.

There was one thing that I could do, however. The money! I could feel the weight of it in my pocket and on my soul. Realising it wasn't all that important, except symbolically, but hating the symbol, hating the material representation of the crime I was now regretting, I went to the chief priests and gave it back to them. I didn't want it, didn't want anything to with it. Jesus was innocent. I was surprised and stunned to find that they didn't want anything to do with the money or me; their contempt was obvious. So I threw it on the ground and got away as quickly as possible. I was so absorbed in returning the money and in Peter's tragedy that I didn't see much of the trial before Annas and Caiaphas, but I went along to the praetorium. Peter had dropped off. Whereas the other Jews wouldn't enter the praetorium, by this time I was becoming bold and almost self-destructive, acting with uncharacteristic recklessness. I had eaten the Passover with Jesus, and so need not have been concerned about defilement. But beyond that, and making it irrelevant, was the thought that I had defiled myself in my betrayal of Jesus to such an extent that ritual defilement of the type feared by the Pharisees was as less than nothing. I went into the praetorium, and witnessed the whole of what happened before Pilate. My mind, by this time, was operating with feverish intensity; my heart was pounding; my senses were heightened. I seemed to record all that was said and all that I saw. I was later to wonder at the total recall I had of what people said and what they did. The nature that was unable to work easily with the apostolic band, which was the opposite in many ways of my friend Peter, made me a good observer; God had given me this talent for a purpose. Years later I could recall with perfect clarity not only words, but a photographic image, of faces and scenes. I was sensitive to what was happening. Because I had been on both sides, I could see both sides, see clearly the hatred of all that is good that motivated those who made themselves Jesus' enemies; I could see the mob psychology which brought to the fore the worst in men, sweeping aside the best, the rational, the loving and forgiving.

Because I had loved, and still did, the Lord, I could see the trial and crucifixion for what it was. I came to appreciate Jesus' calm acceptance of his fate (without having heard that prayer in Gethsemane) and maybe, as much as any human can, I came to understand why Jesus had to die (as I looked into my own soul and saw my own guilt). I recorded all this in its essence, and I recorded some of its irony – the Pharisees unwilling to defile themselves by contamination with the Gentiles (by entering the praetorium), defiling themselves infinitely by killing "The Holy and Righteous One, the Author of Life"; the high priests, so intent upon getting Jesus condemned to death that they shouted, "We have no king but Caesar!" This contradicted the Jews' political convictions of the time and the best of their religious tradition. Other Jews were dying rather than blaspheme, rather than acknowledge to the Romans other than God as their King. I followed the procession up the Via Dolorosa to Golgotha. My description of the crucifixion is stark in its simplicity. I give an actual quotation from Jesus' lips. I make no attempt to embellish or dramatise. It is unnecessary and unfitting. The drama was there without dramatization; the meaning is more than man can comprehend.

I can't begin to define my state of mind at this point except as a highly complex meld of regret, guilt, estrangement, love and awe. Strangely, I didn't feel pity for Jesus. I knew that he didn't need and didn't want that. Even with the blood flowing from his wounds, physically in agony, he was in command. The word, 'Worship' best describes my emotional state. But more important than *my* feelings, *my* emotions, was what was happening to Jesus. I was transfixed, totally absorbed in looking at Jesus, taking it all in, the whole scene. This accounts for the compelling power of my account. I was so fascinated by what was happening before me that, mercifully, I forgot myself; for the moment my own crime and guilt was set aside by the redeeming love I saw before me. This was my salvation and our great benefit. I was at the foot of the cross. I stood there, slightly apart from the group of women, trying to be part of their group, not certain of whether they *knew*. (Had they known?). It was a bare eight hours since I had betrayed Jesus. The disciples had scattered. Had there been time to compare notes, to add the bits and pieces of evidence, to remember that Judas-Beloved Disciple had left the Last Supper, sent by the Lord, that I hadn't been with him in Gethsemane, that I had reappeared mysteriously at the same time the arresting force came for Jesus, that there was that strange scene when I came forward to kiss Jesus? Had Peter had time to think about the ease with which I had been able to get into the house of Ca'iaphas, my apparent

11

familiarity with some of the Sanhedrin, my bizarre and inappropriate behaviour over the last few days.

It wasn't until later when the apostles got together, compared experiences and heard the rumour from the Pharisees that one of the twelve had betrayed him, that the realisation came to them that I was a traitor. I doubt that I was able to conceal, or even wanted to conceal my shame and overwhelming sense of guilt. Mercifully they, too, had more important things to think about than Judas as the drama unfolded before them. So I, Judas-Beloved Disciple, stood at the foot of the cross. So much had happened so recently (the Last Supper; the kiss [or lack of it]; the trial; the return of the money; the long trek to Golgotha). Throughout, the bearing and nobility of Jesus was impressive and in stark contrast to those who had tried to confuse, humiliate and degrade him. The Sanhedrin had flung their arguments at Jesus. I had come to see that they simply were not true. Jesus was not going to start an insurrection, had never had any intention of that, he was not in any way a tool of the Zealots. He was his own man and, in the same person, God's man. It was the Pharisees who were the danger – their hate, their subordination of justice, even of national dignity, their obsequiousness to Pilate in the desire to get Jesus, at any price. His own disciples had failed him. This all came to me repeatedly, run over and over again, in moments of full realisation, and most powerfully and strangely at the moment of Jesus' greatest humiliation, when they lifted his body and hammered the nails in, what came to me then was that it was true. **It was true!** – *all* those things that Jesus had said. "I am the Good Shepherd"; "I am the Bread of Life"; "I am the Way, the Truth and the Life". *Jesus was simply telling the truth.* I was simply wrong, completely and tragically wrong. These were not extravagant claims made by an egotist who had lost touch with reality. Jesus spoke the truth. Any other man with such ideas would have been a dangerous lunatic. Jesus was different. He was, even as he hung there, especially as he hung there, the Son, the word become flesh, the light of the world, even in his misery, he was full of grace and truth. The words came later, in the full light of the resurrection and after many years of prayer and meditation. But the realisation was there then.

Along with it came the guilt. A man can stand just so much. I was shielded from the full impact of what I had done, shielded by the sheer wonder of what I had come to realise, shielded by a sense of the inevitable, that Jesus would have died even if no Judas had been born. But I also sensed enough of the truth of the tragedy to know my own guilt. I needn't feel sorry for Jesus; he had made that clear ("Daughters of Jerusalem, do not weep for me, but weep for yourselves and for your children" Luke 23.28). I was weeping copiously but it was for me and the others. Jesus neither needed nor wanted our pity. Jesus had always been equal to any situation, and was so even on the cross. I realised how completely, how horribly, I had been wrong. Here I had been one of the twelve, one of that inner circle, that close band of apostolic fellowship, privy to Jesus' words and action, privileged to hear what I had heard and see what I had seen, and I had thrown it all away. I was the swine before whom the pearl had been cast. I was in the light and, of my own free will, I had gone out into the dark. I wept.

So I, Judas, the Beloved Disciple, stood there before the cross, in abject misery, hardly daring to look at Jesus' face, wanting to throw myself at Jesus' feet to beg forgiveness, but feeling no confidence that I should even ask it, wanting to edge closer to the women. Surely Mary, his mother, surely Mary Magdalene, would understand, and yet believing that they would never, if they lived a thousand years, understand how, much less, why, I could have betrayed him.

Then it happened. Jesus, his eyes glazed in pain and exhaustion, stirred. Involuntarily, we stepped forward (as if I could help). I looked up into Jesus' face. Mary, his mother, had also stepped forward. Jesus' eyes then focused on us. We were there together when Jesus spoke, softly, but clearly and audibly, **"Woman, behold your son** (and to me) **behold your mother"**.

And it came to me that Jesus knew, even on the cross, in his agony, he knew, and that he had forgiven me. I wept now in relief and joy. My arms went around Mary, her arms around me. I sank to the ground at Jesus' feet, drawing Mary with me. We stayed there for I know not how long. Peace came to me, the peace of God, a peace which was down deep, deeper even than my shame and misery. In establishing the relationship between me and his mother, Jesus had also re-established the relationship between himself and me, that relationship which I had severed. We stayed there until the end when the soldiers pieced his side so we could be with our Lord in his final agony. I wanted to see everything, already having a glimmer of a feeling that I must, somehow, tell others what I was seeing. I was no longer concerned about my own reputation, my own position in the Christian community, or what the others thought. This kind of concern, which was to re-emerge later, was subordinated to my feeling of peace at the miracle of my forgiveness. I was once more a follower, loving the Lord with that early total commitment, trusting entirely in his grace. I was there at Jesus' death. I was there when my friend, Nicodemus, with Joseph, came to take away the body of Jesus. By this time, I was beginning to feel the weight of his guilt, the human consequences of my betrayal; I was questioning my position in the apostolic band. Not knowing what they knew or suspected about the betrayal, not even able to enquire, I found myself standing alone, feeling unworthy and despised by the Pharisees and the disciples alike. Jesus' forgiveness was a miracle, but I couldn't assume the Christian community would accept, or repeat, this forgiveness.

The day that had begun shortly after midnight with my betrayal in the garden, ended with the burial of the Lord, less than eighteen hours afterwards. I was exhausted and went home to sleep, a peaceful sleep bathed in Jesus' forgiveness. When I awoke it was with a strong need to talk with Mary. We had been committed to each other. I had to tell her, to talk it over, to confess to Jesus' mother – and now, by his command, my mother. She was the one to tell, my confessor. I went to Mary and confessed. Mary Magdalene was there but I told both of them the whole sad story. I didn't try to minimize my personal responsibility in the despicable betrayal, although I did express his belief that I was bedevilled. I told how he had repented of my crime, how it had come to me standing at the foot of the cross, how terribly and tragically he had been wrong. I had wanted to ask Jesus for forgiveness, but didn't know if he could hear, didn't know if he could respond. I told of my feelings when Jesus spoke and said those wonderful words which were both a sacred trust and words of forgiveness. Mary was sympathetic; she agreed that I had been forgiven; and came to believe that Jesus had meant her to use her undoubted influence to help me. Mary Magdalene remembered her own cleansing from the devils who inhabited her and she, too, forgave me as much as she could.

Thus it was natural that Mary Magdalene came to me, as well as to Peter, when she found that the tomb was empty. Peter and I were in different places, and hadn't seen each other since I had gained him entry into the high priest's court. Peter had had time to think and he was suspicious of me. But all this was forgotten in the astonishing news that Mary Magdalene delivered. We raced to the tomb together. I got there first, but I didn't go in. Mine was a naturally passive nature, more the spectator than the participant, but I also had an instinctive sense of what was fitting. I should not be the first in the tomb. I deferred to Peter and then he went in and believed.

I still do not know what I did believe at that time. I don't think I realised the full import of the resurrection. But the burial cloths and the napkin, lying there so neatly, were impressed on my consciousness, reminding me of Lazarus coming out of the tomb and of Jesus saying, "I am the resurrection and the life". Perhaps it is most accurate to say that an undifferentiated feeling that all was well came into my heart, my mind, my soul. Death had not prevailed; Jesus lives. I could not possibly believe that it was all over, even after seeing Jesus at the trial and on the cross. I had come to believe absolutely that he was what he said he was. I did not believe that the tomb was the end of him, that he who was so alive could really be gone forever. After the discovery of the empty tomb, Peter and I went back. Peter went to his home and then to the Upper Room to discuss with the others what he had discovered. Was I on the agenda? I went to a growing isolation; I didn't feel it was an appropriate time to burden Mary further.

The next two weeks were difficult ones for me. I imagined my treachery had become known and discussed among the disciples. The question was what to do with me or about me. Mary probably stood up for me and advised waiting for Jesus. Jesus had said I was her son. I didn't know what Peter was thinking. I hadn't seen him since the empty tomb. I didn't join the other apostles. I had an informant, the disciple John, the son of Zebedee. John was sympathetic. He kept me in touch. I told him what Mary and I heard Jesus say on the cross. I had a feeling that he knew already. He kept me informed of what was happening, of how Jesus had appeared to the other eleven.

When some of the disciples went back to Galilee, John let me know, and I trailed along. I told myself that the others had much to answer for at the time of the crucifixion, but I could not pretend that their failures were as monstrous as mine. I was tolerated, and that was something. But the question remained, unspoken and unresolved, "What was going to be done with me?" Should I be punished, even sent back to the Pharisees? Should I be ostracized, become a spiritual leper? Should I be received back into the Christian community?" Nobody wanted to answer the question. They waited.

Then, that glorious moment; they were fishing in Galilee. Someone spoke to us from the shore. I looked and looked more closely. Surely, it looked like him. It was the Lord! Without thinking, I spoke first to Peter, as I would have done in the old days. Peter jumped into the water and swam and we brought the boat in. Hesitantly, hopefully, we gathered around Jesus and had breakfast together. It was a beautiful morning by the lakeside. I heard the dialogue between Jesus and Peter. As they moved off, I followed, hesitantly. I heard Peter ask the question "Lord, what about this man?" Feeling deeply the hardness in Peter's voice, I waited confidently for the reply. Whatever the answer I was satisfied that if the appeal went directly to Jesus. Jesus' answer was that I should remain alive. He didn't tell them they must forgive, or receive him back into the apostolic fellowship. I came to believe that there was a purpose behind that too. From that moment, I realised that I could not stay with the apostolic band. I had one more thing to do. I discharged my responsibilities to Mary, made sure that she would be looked after and taken care of by the apostles. I had time enough to talk with John, son of Zebedee, and to receive further assurance of his sympathy. Then I disappeared. Rumours later circulated, given wings by men's willingness to believe the worst or to make a scapegoat of me for the sins of many, that I was dead, that I had committed suicide, or that I had died a horrible death. I didn't know about this at the time.

I knew I was an enigma to the eleven disciples, an embarrassment to them, and an embarrassment to myself. I saw that I couldn't simply go on like this all my life, tolerated but not accepted, an object of pity to some, treated like an un-person by many, kept a distance as though a spiritual leper by others, a curiosity for strangers. So I did the only thing I could; I dropped out and went underground leaving no clue as to where I went. I disappeared at once and without explanation. I did tell John I was going but I had no idea where I was headed. Like John the Baptist and Jesus I went north into wilderness. I went on retreat. I found safety and sanctuary in a remote area; I holed up, lived in a cave, and foraged for food. I stayed away from people. No one knew who I was. I was totally cut off from my former life. I stayed holed up for a few years and then migrated from my cave to Asia Minor, staying off the beaten paths, so I wouldn't be recognized, and working by slow stages toward one of the Greek cities of Asia Minor or the Black Sea where there was little likelihood that I would be recognized. Here I was able to get writing materials and produce **The Judas Gospel.** Here I also came in contact with Greek thought and gnostic teaching which I was able to use (*not* the other way around) in the first chapter of the Fourth Gospel. While in the vicinity I heard that the apostle John was nearby, famous by now as about the only of the original twelve known to be still living, the others having long since gone to the corners of the world to spread the word and to die in so doing. I needed a city, a non Christian community, to pursue my aim in life. The other disciples had their mission. I had my unique calling – to write down what I had seen, what I was an eyewitness to, some of which I, alone, knew about Jesus. I came to believe this with a great passion. This something was that I had in me, in my heart, in my mind, a very special treasure for the Christian world. I had always been a sensitive observer, one with a memory for detail and conversation, and one who saw not only what happened but had an awareness of the deeper implications. I am articulate and literate. There were things that only I had seen about Jesus, things that only I knew. This must not be lost! I came to believe that this might have been what Jesus saw in me from the beginning, the reason Jesus chose me, the only Judean, as one of the Twelve. Was this what he had in mind for me, the purpose for which he spared, ransomed, healed, restored and forgave me? Yes! This grew into the dominant conviction of my life. My life had been one of thanksgiving for Jesus' forgiveness. It determined all that I did, the future course of my life. It was my mission; my chance to repay Jesus' trust. The other disciples had their holy orders; I had mine. I regretted that I couldn't be with them as before, but my isolation was necessary. I would write it all down (not all) but what I could. I would produce a book, a Gospel, another account of the good news in Jesus Christ. Mark, Matthew, Luke had done this. The Christians world had seen the value of these; they had been copied and passed along time after time. These Gospels were of inestimable value to the emerging church as many who had been eyewitnesses were no longer alive. I would have to get my memoirs down in writing. But how? And then, blessed moment, I heard on the grapevine that John the apostle was alive and ministering in Ephesus and the surrounding area. When I heard he was coming nearby to preach, I made discrete contact, making sure he was entirely alone when I met him. I explained the situation and he enthusiastically agreed to help. We spent many hours alone; I showed him what I had done; and we sketched out a plan of action. He had a group of disciples in Ephesus who could help. John agreed that we couldn't reveal my identity because that might prejudice them. I was still a pariah. So, we arranged to give him what I had written and for me to get him more as we went on. I had been thinking about it for years when I was in the cave; I had even organized it in my mind and now it was a matter of getting it all down on papyrus. We worked like this for a year or so. I got batches of material to him, always anonymously. He edited the material, turned it over to his disciples, and they reworked it. Then it came back to me for another editing. This soon became cumbersome, so we decided I would surface, introduced simply as a friend and additional disciple of John. I stayed with them so I could be closer to the task. We still had to be careful not to reveal my identity; we were just close friends. I found him a man of great faith and keen intelligence; he had written several letters of his own to friends, which had been copied and circulated throughout the Christian world; he was a good editor and I needed that because I could have written volumes; he was much in demand as a pastor and teacher and eyewitness to Jesus' ministry; in spite of this, he gave generously of his time and we spent precious hours together working out that document which became the Fourth Gospel; we merged our memories of Jesus and our insights and he made a significant contribution. I stayed with him and his community and rejoiced at being restored to the apostolic fellowship; I was still only known as a friend. Some of his people may have had their suspicions about me but they never surfaced and we dared not entrust even them with our secret. The Fourth Gospel went out under John's name, ensuring it would get a hearing on its merits. I could ask for no more. I had accomplished the task assigned to me by Jesus. I am saying "thank you Jesus".

B. **The Problem**

I realised that if my message were going to be received I must be very shrewd. The very early Christian community was not concerned with written reports, they listened to what people had to say about Jesus. The Gospel was first "kerygma", a preached message. What they wanted were eyewitness accounts, not what somebody said somebody had said. This made it very difficult for me. I was an eyewitness, but who would listen (without prejudice) to what I had to say? I could see a time coming when written accounts would not only be acceptable but would be a necessity. I saw this time as being the time when my contribution could be made and appreciated.

However, verbal or written, the difficulty remained. The best accreditation would be that of an eyewitness, and yet I couldn't risk my Gospel by declaring myself, even years, or decades after the event. Further, a Gospel couldn't be dropped out of the blue on the Church. It had to come from somewhere, had to have some port of origin,[1] it had to originate from a person with access to a network, preferably a person of unquestioned integrity and status. The apostle John was perfect for this purpose.

The problem, then was two-fold. *First*, how to write my Gospel, making it clear that this was first-hand, apostolic information of the highest reliability, without showing my hand. *Second*, how to launch my Gospel from some credible Christian base, without, again, disclosing the ultimate source of the information.

I Judas, the Beloved Disciple, had time to think about this. I disappeared from sight. Did I go into the desert, as Browning imagines *"A Death in the Desert"*, or did I go far away? At any rate, I disappeared from sight, so completely that I could be assumed dead.   **Amen**

---

[1] It is relevant to object at this point that if Judas thought this necessary for his Gospel to have credibility (i.e. that it be accepted as eyewitness and that it have respectable credentials) then why do we know so little about the authors of the other Gospels and why are they not more emphatic about being eyewitness accounts. The answer is that the Synoptics came into being in a different way. They are (demonstrably) more dependent upon other sources (For instance neither Matthew nor Luke, was likely to have been present at Jesus' birth). They are earlier. Since it was apparent to the early Christian community that they had come out of the community there was less question of doubting their authenticity, or of attaching more than a name to the manuscript. The continuity between oral tradition and the written Gospel was well-established and apparent. The situation with the Fourth Gospel was different.

C.1. **Solution to the Problem**

To repeat, the problem was two-fold:

First, Judas had to establish his credentials as an eyewitness without disclosing his identity. There were the following possibilities:

(1) He could simply put his pseudonym on the "title" page, perhaps with an explanation that the author was an eyewitness of what followed. The objection to this was that it would be bound to cause a mystery from the beginning. The question would be asked, "Who was this author? Who knew him, or of him?" Since there was no ready explanation, either the reader might be excused for concluding that the author wasn't an eyewitness, or that he had something to hide. Also, and more important to the author's purpose, the eyewitness should be placed in the Gospel narrative in such a position that the importance of his testimony was obvious to the reader in the reading. Title pages and ascriptions get misplaced or are not noticed by the reader who doesn't start at the beginning sometimes. Manuscripts get mixed up in transmission and copying. Judas had been in the Upper Room, at the trial, the crucifixion and at the empty tomb. This was what he had to offer. But he couldn't place himself there as eyewitness and author without giving away his real identity if he told the story the way he felt it must be told.

(2) He could use the pseudonym throughout, substituting some other name for Judas. The objections to this were (a) that there was one incident where everyone would have known that the anonymous author was Judas – the betrayer. It would not be long before everyone knew the betrayer was Judas, and that would give away the authorship. (b) There were other places (e.g. the trials) where there were people present too numerous to be accounted for and too young to have been been assumed dead by the time the Gospel was released who could have concluded that the anonymous eyewitness had to be Judas.

(3) This meant that he had to use a combination of pseudonym and "Judas". That is, he had to use "Judas" in those places where there were people apt to be alive who could have identified the anonymous eyewitness as Judas and therefore given away the authorship. But he could use the pseudonym in *selected places* where he had reason to know that the other participants were either dead by the time the Gospel was released or would keep quiet. Thus he could show that the eyewitness was present at critical points without disclosing that it was Judas.

C.2 **A Pseudonym**

Having concluded this, Judas had to decide upon a pseudonym. It had to be a name which could not be connected with Judas. That was important. It could not be a nickname, a name that had been used for him, or a play on names. It could not be a proper name, because, for instance in the Upper Room, the proper names of the twelve disciples were commonly known. To introduce another name would have been readily discernible as inaccurate (by commonsense and by comparison to the Synoptics) and so discredit the whole of the account. So it must be a name which would surely preserve the anonymity of the author, not a proper name, and not one which would be applied to any of the other disciples; and, if possible, a name which described or established the close relationship Judas had with Jesus (without, of course, making the identification obvious or even logical).

C.3 **Beloved Disciple**

The name, Beloved Disciple (or reference to, the disciple whom Jesus loved) fits these requirements. It is not a proper name, it was not used by Jesus or Judas. It would not, therefore, connect with Judas the eyewitness even, necessarily, in the disciples' minds. It establishes a close relationship between the author and Jesus, *without saying that the relationship was exclusive* (i.e. that he loved only that disciple, or loved him more than the others, neither of which was true).

It utilises a basic word, *the* basic word, in the Christian vocabulary (and in the Johannine vocabulary) and therefore the name itself reinforced the credibility of the eyewitness. There was an additional subtlety in the text of the Gospel of John, the author was able to use the basic word of the Christian vocabulary, <u>love</u> in the Greek ἀγαπάω to refer to the Beloved Disciple, John also uses this Greek word in combination with another but nearer Greek word for love, driving home the point. The author was able to use the words (φιλέω and ἀγαπάω), Jesus used these in his last, so important, conversation with Peter. Thus Judas established in an almost subliminal way the connection with Peter and the similarity of their positions in the apostolic band.

D. **How to Solve It**

Now Judas set his mind to where he must use "Judas" and where he could use the pseudonym, "the disciple whom Jesus loved". As the author says (21:25) he made a selection of material to include in his Gospel from a much larger amount of material. We can imagine that Judas found it necessary to discard some material where it would have been difficult to use either "Judas" or "Beloved Disciple". For instance, if there had been a conversation between Jesus and Judas alone but observed by others (which might well have happened) he couldn't have included it because, if he used *Judas* the question would have been asked, "What was the source?" and a connection might be established with the author. As it was, he slipped up by showing a knowledge of what was in Judas' mind, or was this intended? If he used the "Beloved Disciple" there might have been some who had observed the conversation without hearing it who could have made the identification. Whether that is the case or not, he must have been careful as to how he used his own name and the pseudonym. Let us see how this was done.

The following summary of incidents in which Judas and/or Beloved Disciple are used will help:

Summary of Incidents and Passages in which Judas and/or Beloved Disciple are used

Fourth Gospel	Judas	Beloved Disciple	"another disciple"
6:71	Betrayal Forecast		
12:1-8	Anointing of Jesus by Mary		
13	Upper Room	Upper Room	
18:2-12	Gethsemane		
18:15ff	Betrayal		High Priest's Court (Peter's Denial)
19:25-27		During the Crucifixion	
20:1-6		The Empty Tomb	
21		Resurrection by the Sea of Tiberias	

He used *Judas* in the four incidents in which Judas appears and is identified as such (6:71; 12:1-8,13; 18:2-12) for similar but slightly different reasons. To start, it was necessary for Judas to appear, by name, because he was an important actor in the drama, independent of his own feelings in the matter. Obviously, it would not have been possible for him not to appear by name in the Garden of Gethsemane. It follows that he chose to include Jesus' forecast of his betrayal because this forecast was an important moment in his own life and important in setting the scene for what happened later (Upper Room and Betrayal). The next incident (the anointing of Jesus by Mary) was not vital to the story. To be certain, it gave insight into Judas' character and perhaps he thought it went part way to explain his moral disintegration, to expose the fact that he had been stealing; avarice leads to petty thievery leads to cover-up leads to a major crime. I have seen this progression with a Church Warden, a Church Treasurer and a C. of E. clergyman. Another possible reason for including the Anointing was that it cast Mary in a favourable light. If Mary were Mary Magdalene and if she and Judas were good friends (although that may be at least one too many contingencies) then there would be a reason for including it for her sake. His good name was lost to posterity in any case; compared to the betrayal, his actions here were of trivial importance.

When it came to the Upper Room, Judas had a different problem. His role, as Judas, the traitor, was too important for him to leave out altogether. Also, if he had reported all that happened, including the question by Peter, his repetition of the question to Jesus, and Jesus' answer, the way it happened, then it would have been apparent to the careful reader that since Judas was the only one who had that information he must have been the source of it, and a connection might have been made with authorship. On the other hand, he was concerned to begin to assert in important incidents in the Passion story, that his was an eyewitness account. Also, his account of the Last Supper differed substantially from the Synoptic account and recorded important information that they didn't (e.g. the foot washing). It was important to him to show that his material (at least the material in Chapter 13, before Judas left) had eyewitness authority.

Therefore, in <u>this scene alone</u>, the Upper Room, he had two somewhat opposed designs. He must have *Judas*, and he wanted very much to have the *Beloved Disciple* as eyewitness. If he had *Judas* alone, then he would be giving an important clue to the authorship. He couldn't have *Beloved Disciple* alone, unless he was willing to leave out the whole of the conversation around the table in 13:21-30. He solved this in a very ingenious way, by leaving the name *Judas* wherever possible, but substituting "Beloved Disciple" in the query from Peter relayed to Jesus. To demonstrate this, the conversation makes good sense if we assume that the Beloved Disciple is *Judas*, and drop the pseudonym:

"When Jesus had thus spoken, he was troubled in spirit, and testified, 'Truly, truly, I say to you, one of you will betray me'. The disciples looked at one another, uncertain of whom he spoke. Judas was lying close to the breast of Jesus; so Simon Peter beckoned to him and said, 'Tell us who it is of whom he speaks'. So lying thus, close to the breast of Jesus, Judas said to him, 'Lord, who is it?' Jesus answered, 'It is he to whom I shall give this morsel when I have dipped it.' So when he had dipped the morsel, he gave it to Judas", etc.

The fact that the disciples obviously didn't know who the traitor was after this exchange is to be explained by the fact that "lying close to Jesus' breast" the conversation was private in the sense the others could not hear what was said.

By using the pseudonym, Beloved Disciple, in the Upper Room and claiming authorship for this figure later on, he was able to tie down the fact of the eyewitness nature of his information.

The same general considerations apply to the other places where he refers to the disciple whom Jesus loved. That is, each was an important event in the Gospel where he was specially concerned to establish the eyewitness aspect of his evidence. And each was a situation where the people present were either (at the time of transmission of the Gospel to the wider church) known to be dead and so silent. Mary was presumably dead (or we would have heard more about her in early church annals or traditions). Thus there was no one left who could say with any confidence that the person designated "Beloved Disciple" was Judas. This was true at the crucifixion where Mary, the mother of Jesus, was the only other person who heard clearly Jesus' words to her and the Beloved Disciple. It was true at the Empty Tomb where Mary Magdalene and Peter were the Beloved Disciple's two companions. If we wonder at the fact that Peter would not have reported that he and Judas went to the tomb at Mary's bidding, then we must note that Peter doesn't appear to have reported that he went to the tomb at all. This is true of the information we have in the Synoptics, his speeches in Acts and the Epistles ascribed to him. He refers to Judas' betrayal, and the resurrection, both essential in the early kerygma.

The above analysis has left out (18:15) where the author refers to "another disciple". We have assumed all along with many commentators that the Beloved Disciple is the one referred to. We have to ask here why the author didn't use either "Judas" or "Beloved Disciple". The only answer is that there must have been some disadvantage in either, and he needed to confuse the issue a bit. It would have been difficult to use "Beloved Disciple" because there might have been people there who were not accounted for who make the association with Judas. There doesn't seem to be any reason why he couldn't have used "Judas", except perhaps that to use "Judas" might have identified him as the primary source of the information on Peter's denial and therefore discredited his account of the trial before the high priests which differs in emphasis from that of the Synoptics.

E. The Final Hurdle: Getting a "publisher" credible with the Christian Community

Sometime in those years, of anonymity and security, Judas managed to "leak" or to "float" an early manuscript. It is amazing that after 2,000 years THE JUDAS GOSPEL has surfaced, see Chapter VIII. Manuscripts were rife in the first century, copied and recopied, circulated and recirculated. There were many "Gospels". He bided his time, he waited for God to reveal the time and place.

Judas' next problem was to find a base from which to launch his Gospel. He couldn't just write it up and post it to the brethren and expect to have them take it seriously. He had to have some backing. Judas wandered for a long time, many years. He went first to places where he wouldn't be recognised. He was thought to be dead, and as the years went by, he became less and less recognisable even to those who might have recognised him. During these years of his life, which might have been bleak and lonely, he sustained himself with the knowledge that he had something important to impart. It was the all-consuming passion of his life. He would have to wait until the Christian Church had the need for written Gospels and wait until he found the means to transmit it without risk of contamination by discovery of its ultimate source. Judas bided his time and waited years for God to show him the way. It came. He heard that John, the disciple, his friend, was in Ephesus. It had been a long time. He gambled that John would welcome him and not expose him. He could argue that if Jesus had forgiven him, then John should also. No one else would recognise him. He went to John, identified himself, told him of his project, got his approval and backing. John was made aware of the absolute necessity of keeping Judas' identity a closed secret. As far as John's circle knew, this stranger had come out of the wilderness with this wonderful document. John had a circle of disciples. Although Judas' true identity was not revealed to anyone but John, they all worked on making copies and editing the Gospel. It was ascribed, for reasons of caution, and with a certain rough accuracy, to John. He acted as Editor-in-Chief. He was honoured to have his name on it. The sequence was complete. Judas (Beloved Disciple) John.

Judas went back in the wilderness, at peace with himself, secure in God's forgiveness and confident that he had completed his life work, the task that Jesus had given him. He and John remained lifelong friends.

THE ANSWER TO THE WHO QUESTION HAS TO BE JUDAS

This is not entirely an original idea; as impressive, knowledgeable a scholar as William Barclay speculated that this might be the case.

Chapter II

Fourth Gospel References
to Beloved Disciple
Who was the Beloved Disciple?[1]

In this section, we consider the mysterious figure in the Fourth Gospel of the "Beloved Disciple," who appears in the following incidents:

(A) The Upper Room (13:21-30)
(B) The Crucifixion (19:25-27)

The author's resurrection theology

The following needs to be emphasised in the consideration of the resurrection appearances in (C) and (D) below:

(1) These are treated as *literary* documents and reflect the experience(s) and belief(s) of the author(s) of the Fourth Gospel. This is the case, and true, whether or not the reader accepts the primary thesis of the author of this book that the Fourth Gospel was written by Judas in collaboration with John.

(2) The Fourth Gospel has the same inner contradictions as the other Gospels in its account of the resurrection, namely:

In John 20.1-10 the tomb is empty but shows signs of occupancy
In John 20.19-30 Jesus appears to the disciples twice through "shut doors"
In John 20.19-29 Thomas is recorded as being convinced by being invited to place his hands in the wounds..

The resurrection is the central Jesus mystery. The Gospels simply define that mystery. The boundaries of belief are set by a) those who believe that a dead body came to life "God can do anything" and b) those scholars – some Jesus seminar – who do not believe that the Jesus as portrayed in the Gospels existed in the flesh. The author of this book does not believe it is necessary, or possible, to unravel this mystery (certainly not in this book; two lesser mysteries are enough!) I believe passionately in the resurrection, but I do not believe that our Lord's dead body came physically to life after having bled to death and having his side pierced by a sword. We "know" the risen Lord every Sunday. I take great comfort in Jesus' prescient words, speaking to us across 20 centuries. "Blessed are those who have not seen and yet believe" John 20.29

---

[1] Richard Bauckham, author, *Jesus and the Eyewitnesses* (Eerdmans, Grand Rapids, Michigan, 2006

(C) The Empty Tomb (20:1-10)

(D) Resurrection Appearance by the Sea of Tiberias (21).

In addition, an unnamed disciple ("another disciple") appears in John 18:15,16, who could be the Beloved Disciple.

These incidents, including the last, are considered below:

(E) Catalogue of Disciples

(F) The Other Disciple

(G) The Unnamed Disciple

(H) Summary of Chapter II

(A) *The Upper Room.* 13:21-30. This has been examined in the section on references to Judas in Chapter III. In addition it might also be noted that (1) the author makes clear in his recording of this incident the special position of the Beloved Disciple. We see this in the account of the juxtaposition at the table next to Jesus, "lying close to the breast of Jesus".

We also see it in the fact that Peter asks his question about the betrayer through the Beloved Disciple. (2) Here, as in all the incidents in which the Beloved Disciple figures (except at the Cross), Peter and the Beloved Disciple are in conjunction.

(B) *The Crucifixion.* 19:25-27. Standing by the cross of Jesus were his mother, and his mother's sister, Mary the wife of Clopas, and Mary Magdalene. When Jesus saw his mother, and the disciple whom he loved standing near, he said to his mother, "Woman, behold your son!" Then he said to the disciple, "Behold your mother!" "And from that hour the disciple took her to his own home". Now this incident would seem to be a great stumbling block to any identification of Judas as the Beloved Disciple, and for several reasons. The first is that we commonly think of Judas as having vanished from the scene after Gethsemane, publically exposed as the traitor and condemned by the disciples and Jesus. But I have attempted to show that this was not necessarily the case and that in the confusion and emotion of the arrest it was not clear (except by hindsight which coloured the Synoptic accounts as surely as it prejudices our thinking) that Judas was the traitor. If he had not been fully exposed by this time (remembering that it was only hours between the betrayal and the crucifixion; the disciples had scattered and had no opportunity to exchange information, ideas, impressions or judgements) there is no reason to suppose that he was banished from the community at this time. Probably he was running a risk being at the Cross, but had decided his life and reputation weren't worth much at this point and what had he to lose? He may have felt an overwhelming desire to be with the Lord he loved (certainly he who was loved

Italian Crucifix

The Rev. Edward Downing was a padre with a British Parachute Regiment as they fought their way up the Italian Peninsula in WW2. On Christmas Eve he found himself near a barn where cattle were stabled. He celebrated Communion with the troops, accompanied by smells and sounds of the cattle; the most impressive setting of all his Christmas Eve Masses. He recovered this crucifix about the same time and much later gave it to us.

27

Cross hanging over the altar at the Parish Church of Christ Church,
Davyhulme, Diocese of Manchester.

This cross was made of perspex and oak by Josefina de Vasconcellos working with young men on remand and was given to the parish through the good offices of The Rev. Edward Downing. Prior to this it has been hanging in St. Martin in the Fields, London. The shadow behind the cross appears on the east wall of the church. Under the usual lighting during worship, two shadows are visible, reminding worshippers of the two criminals crucified with Jesus. Thus the cross as pictured can be seen as presenting the crucified and the risen Lord. (see Luke 23:33).

by the Lord must have reciprocated) regardless of the risk and even though he had betrayed him.

Another major objection posed by this section to the identification of Judas with the Beloved Disciple is that we might be inclined to doubt that Jesus would place his mother in the charge of the one who betrayed him, and vice versa. For one thing there would be practical difficulties, i.e. would Judas, on the run after the Crucifixion, have been able to do this. But here, to go back to the text,[2] Jesus didn't place his mother in the Beloved Disciple's hands, or vice versa. From what he said ("Woman, behold your son" . . . "Behold your mother") we can only know that he was establishing a relationship, a relationship which he knew would be beneficial to either one or the other or to both. We infer that the Beloved Disciple was to provide Mary with a home because the later part of verse 27 is "And from that hour the disciple took her to his own home". But is that what the phrase means? The phrase εἰς τὰ ἴδια is used three times by John.[3] The first of these is 1:11 ("He came to his own home, and his own people received him not"). Obviously, what is thought of here is not "his own place of residence," but "his own people". The second place is 16:32 ("The hour is coming, indeed it has come, when you will be scattered, every man to his home . . ."). Here the home is seen as "place of refuge". Looked at in this light, what the Beloved did was to take Mary to his own self as his own mother. "From that hour" then can be taken to mean both that he took her (mercifully) from the scene of the crucifixion (from the final stages of her son's dying agony), that he accepted the commission to have her for his own mother, from that time.

The description of the group at the cross infers that there was the group of women, with the Beloved Disciple a short distance away (otherwise why not simply include the Beloved Disciple with the group of women). This might indicate that they had distanced themselves from the Beloved Disciple. It would indicate to Jesus on the cross at a glance the nature of the situation (the growing isolation of the Beloved Disciple from the Christian community).

Jesus here addresses his mother as "Woman" other than "Mother". The reason could be that having come into His Kingdom what he has to say is not addressed to her as a human son as much as the Divine Lord of all. It was not a request made by a son to his mother, it was a command within the context of the obedience of a disciple to the Lord Jesus.

---

[2] R. E. Brown, *The Gospel According to John*, pages 922-27 has his usual thorough and illuminating discussion of this incident.

[3] ICC, John page 637. (John 1:11, 16:32, 19:27).

We can reconstruct the following based upon what is said above.

Jesus, in his agony, looked down from the cross and saw the Beloved Disciple–Judas standing there with the small group of women. Realizing by his presence at the scene of the crucifixion (as well as knowing him, as he knows us all so well) that Judas–Beloved Disciple had repented or was ambivalent about his betrayal, Jesus forgave him or trusted him yet again. Can we believe that he would do less? (Matthew 18:22). Forgiving him he went one step further, or, rather, made his forgiveness evident in an action (typically) by having him take his place as son, that is, having his mother adopt him. This was a two-way street. For Mary was specially placed to protect Judas–Beloved Disciple and this may be why Jesus did it.

We would assume that Mary was given a son to protect her. But it could be it was not for Mary's but the Beloved Disciple's sake. Within the Christian community Mary was in a strong position. The Beloved Disciple needed protecting (Mary was the person who in such a matter was placed to have more influence than anyone else). Was Jesus here evoking the maternal instinct?

This act of Jesus on the cross could have saved Judas–Beloved Disciple from the hostility or estrangement or persecution by the early Christian community when they came to sort things out after the resurrection and realized exactly what had happened at Gethsemane. Perhaps they had, or would, find a measure of forgiveness for him themselves. In any case if my hypothesis holds, this is a wonderful evidence of our Lord's compassion even in his agony on the cross. It fits in with Jesus' concern for the Beloved Disciple evidenced in those otherwise mysterious and inexplicable words at the end of the Gospel (21:20-23).

One final point. If Jesus had publically forgiven Judas in this way, would not this have made such an impact on the early Christian community as to have had some reflection in the Gospels or in tradition? One would think so, and yet, we see the kind of emotional trauma that surrounded events at this time. We need to examine the situation and the disciples' mental state at this time. There was much confusion, little time for comparing experiences, gathering facts. The disciples were scattered, stunned by their grief.

Jesus had eaten the Passover meal with his disciples, been betrayed, tried and crucified, all in less than 24 hours.[4] There was much to assimilate. Compare the emotions of many today who lose a loved one in death. There is a period, often lasting for longer than 24 hours, of stunned disbelief, a cessation of normal reasoning. Certainly this would have represented the state of mind of Jesus'

---

[4] Westcott, page 250. Westcott approximates his betrayal at 1.00 a.m. and his death at 3.00 p.m. *The Gospel According to St. John*, B. F. Westcott.

followers at this time. They had other things to think about than Judas, traitor or forgiven penitent. They had their own guilt to deal with – Peter his denials, the others hadn't even gone that far in following the arrested Jesus.

The early Christian community were not concerned with other people – their concern was with Jesus. Likewise the Gospels were not concerned with setting the record straight as far as the minor actors in the drama were concerned, their concern was with the Good News.

There must have been plenty that was left out as the author himself acknowledges (21.25). Still the feeling persists that this would have been preserved somewhere if known. The answer to that is that there is no need to believe it was. No other evangelist records the commendation of Mary to the Beloved Disciple and the Beloved Disciple to Mary. Surely they would have if it had been generally known. Jesus was weak, his speech was perhaps slurred and certainly misunderstood at one point (Mark 15:33-41). Luke makes a special point of saying that he cried with a loud voice (Luke 23:46) perhaps contrasting this with his other utterances. The crucifixion stretched over six hours. It is unlikely that the same people remained in the same positions for all that time. Jesus may have spoken to Mary and the Beloved Disciple in such a way as was not heard or understood by the others. Mary, as the mother, and the Beloved Disciple, can readily be pictured as being nearest the cross. The author of the Fourth Gospel doesn't feel it is necessary to explain in at least one other instance (13:21-30) that what was said to the Beloved Disciple couldn't be heard by the others (and in that case the conversation couldn't have been overheard). So it is possible that these words were heard by Mary and the Beloved Disciple–Judas alone.

The Synoptic Gospels place the group of women at the crucifixion at the time of death "looking on from far". John has the group of women "standing by" the cross near the beginning of the crucifixion. There is a question about the names of the women, but the fact that concerns this study is that the Fourth Gospel names Jesus' mother, while the Synoptics do not list her. An explanation for this could be as follows. The group of women (Mary, the mother of Jesus included) stood near to the Cross (as might have been Mary's prerogative as mother of the crucified)[5]. After Jesus' words to them (19:26 & 27) the Beloved Disciple-Judas took Mary home (or at least away) from the scene of the crucifixion. The women (without Mary's support or justification for being there) retreat to the background (where they are observed and placed by the

---

[5] See Brown p. 904 where he cites E. Stauffer *Jesus and History* to the effect that "the crucified was often surrounded by relatives, friends and enemies during the long hours of this agonizing penalty".

Synoptics). The Beloved–Disciple Judas returns to the scene but misses some of what has happened. This partially explains incidents recorded by the Synoptics but not by the Fourth Gospel.

(C) *The Empty Tomb* (20:1-10)[6]

> Now on the first day of the week Mary Magdalene came to the tomb early, while it was still dark, and saw that the stone had been taken away from the tomb. So she ran, and went to Simon Peter and other disciple, the one whom Jesus loved, and said to them, "They have taken the Lord out of the tomb, and we do not know where they have laid him". Peter then came out with the *other disciple*, and they went toward the tomb. They both ran, but the *other disciple* outran Peter and reached the tomb first; and stooping to look in, he saw the linen cloths lying there, but he did not go in. Then Simon Peter came, following him, and he went into the tomb; he saw the linen cloths lying, and the napkin, which had been on his head, not lying with the linen cloths but rolled up in a place by itself. Then the other disciple, who reached the tomb first, also went in, and he saw and believed; for as yet they did not know the scripture, that he must rise from the dead. Then the disciples went back to their homes.

Mary Magdalene went first to the tomb. If, as older commentators and even at least one modern commentator (Bernard)[7] believe, Mary Magdalene and Mary of Bethany are the same, then we have an association between her and Judas–Beloved Disciple (of Bethany). Judas was, of course, present at the anointing by Mary (12:1-9); the Beloved Disciple and Mary Magdalene were together at the foot of the cross (19:25-26). So it would be natural that to report the empty tomb she would go to Peter (as still the spokesman of the disciples, even after his denial) and to the Beloved Disciple with whom she had been drawn into close association. This also would have had to involve a reconciliation between her and Judas after his unkind words about the anointing. Perhaps Judas learned through the rebuke by Jesus and, because of this, made his peace with Mary. Stranger things have happened. There were two women in a staid Anglican parish church who had had a falling out (one had hit the other's child in Sunday School, of all places!) Both attended a Sunday morning Eucharist at which the gospel included Matthew 5:25. Following the

---

[6] Here the word used for loved is ἐφίλει, in the other references to the Beloved Disciple it is ἠγάπα. Westcott (p. 289). An interchange of two words (although in different context) and that "it is of no fundamental significance". See also Bultmann p. 488.

[7] Referred to in Brown, page 981.

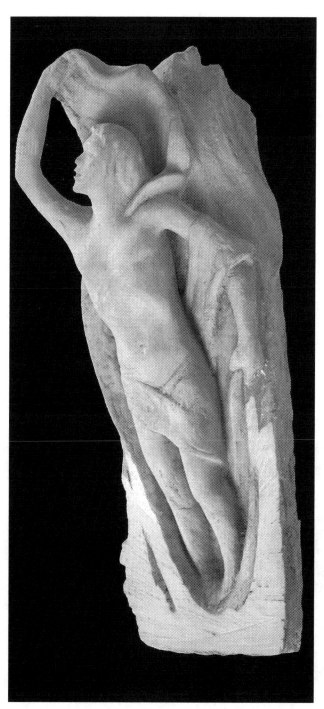

Christ Awakening in the Tomb by Josefina de Vasconcellos

Josefina gave this small sculpture (14 inches long) to us on one of our last visits. I enquired about her current projects (she was in her 99th year). She asked me to go in the next room and bring what I saw there. She then told my wife and me that it was "Christ Awakening in the Tomb". "This has never before been done in the history of Christian art", she said. She gave the sculpture (pictured) to us. Josefina's *modus operandi* was to make a small sculpture as a model for a later, almost life-size sculpture. She didn't live long enough to make the larger sculpture of Christ awakening in the tomb. We have loaned the sculpture to several churches where it has been the focus of meditation on the nature of Christ's resurrection. The nakedness of the figure makes us uneasy; we want him to be clothed. What was the nature of Christ's resurrection? This sculpture answers some questions and raises others. But it is moving, as is all her work. A good focus for meditation about the resurrection of Our Lord.

We keep faith with Josefina by making it available on request to anyone who can assure us that it will be seen and kept safe.

service, the one woman went up to the other quoting the Gospel ("So if you are offering your gift at the altar, and there remember that your brother has something against you, leave your gift there before the altar and go; first be reconciled to your brother; and then come and offer your gift" Matthew 5:25). It was done in public, much to the embarrassment of the second woman, but it happened and worked. They have been friends since. It isn't really much of a venture in faith to speculate that Judas was ashamed of himself, repented, made his amends with Mary Magdalene, and they became close friends, as people can do after a reconciliation.

There is support in the Greek text (the repetition of the word προς (20:12 indicates two homes) for the supposition that Mary had to go to two homes, that Peter and the Beloved Disciple were in different places. If so, it makes it more significant in the sense that she felt it desirable to go to *these two* men. Peter can be explained as natural leader of the apostolic band, but she must have felt it was important also to inform the Beloved Disciple (because of his special position?) Peter must have felt it was important to wait for the Beloved Disciple (because of a personal friendship or because of his importance?) Either the truth about who betrayed Jesus hadn't dawned, or was only a suspicion, or had been accepted in some sense by the community, or Peter and Beloved Disciple/Judas were bound together by their conspicuous failure. If so it was a strange threesome – Mary, thought to have been a prostitute, Peter, who had just denied three times that he knew Jesus, the Beloved Disciple Judas, who had betrayed him.

In passing, it is worth mentioning that there has been a difference of opinion as to whether the identification of the Beloved Disciple in 20:2 (. . . "the other disciple, the one whom Jesus loved") connects the Beloved Disciple with "other disciple" of 18:15 who accompanies Peter to the High Priests.[8]

Peter and the Beloved Disciple ran to the tomb. The Beloved Disciple won the race, but he didn't enter. Why? Could it be that he deferred to Peter as the natural leader of the disciples? Could it be that he was afraid of what he might find? Could it be that he deferred to Peter because of his own sense of unworthiness after the betrayal?

We are next told that the Beloved Disciple entered and that he saw and believed. ἐπίστευσεν What did he believe? Some commentators say that he believed that Mary had told the truth about the body being removed. Other commentators[9] say that he believed that Jesus had risen from the dead. If the latter, then he was the first, and was able to believe on less material evidence

---

[8] See Bultmann, page 645 an also section of John 18:15 following.
[9] See Brown, page 987 for a discussion, also Dodd, page 179-186 on ἐπίστευσεν.

The Resurrection Appearance by The Sea of Tiberias John 21:7.
That disciple whom Jesus loved said to Peter, "It is the Lord!"

than Thomas (and therefore in a position more comparable to our own). It would be ironic if this perception and honour were to have fallen to Judas, but true to the love and redemptive power of Christ.

(D) *The Resurrection Appearance By the Sea of Tiberias* (21)

After this Jesus revealed himself again to the disciples by the Sea of Tiberias; and he revealed himself in this way. Simon Peter, Thomas called the Twin, Nathanael of Cana in Galilee, the sons of Zebedee, and two others of his disciples were together. Simon Peter said to them, "I am going fishing". They said to him, "We will go with you". They went out and got into the boat; but that night they caught nothing.

Just as day was breaking, Jesus stood on the beach; yet the disciples did not know that it was Jesus. Jesus said them, "Children, have you any fish?" They answered him, "No". He said to them, "Cast the net on the right side of the boat, and you will find some". So they cast it, and now they were not able to haul it in, for the quantity of fish. That disciple whom Jesus loved said to Peter, "It is the Lord!" When Simon Peter heard that it was the Lord, he put on his clothes, for he was stripped for work, and sprang into the sea. But the other disciples came in the boat, dragging the net full of fish, for they were not far from the land, but about a hundred yards off.

When they got out on land, they saw a charcoal fire there, with fish lying on it, and bread. Jesus said to them, "Bring some of the fish that you have just caught". So Simon Peter went aboard and hauled the net ashore, full of large fish, a hundred and fifty-three of them; and although there were so many, the net was not torn. Jesus said to them. "Come and have breakfast". Now none of the disciples dared ask him, "Who are you?" They knew it was the Lord. Jesus came and took the bread and gave it to them, and so with the fish. This was now the third time that Jesus was revealed to the disciples after he was raised from the dead.

When they had finished breakfast, Jesus said to Simon Peter, "Simon, son of John, do you love me more than these?" He said to him, "Yes, Lord; you know that I love you". He said to him, "Feed my lambs". A second time he said to him, "Simon, son of John, do you love me?" He said to him, "Yes, Lord; you know that I love you". He said to him, "Tend my sheep". He said to him the third time, "Simon, son of John, do you love me?" Peter was grieved because he said to him the third time, "Do you love me?" And he said to him, "Lord, you know everything; you know that I love you". Jesus said to him, "Feed my sheep. Truly, truly, I say to you, when you were young, you girded yourself and walked where you would, but when you are old, you will stretch out your hands, and another will gird you and carry you where you do not wish to go". (This he said to show by what death he was to glorify God.) And after this he said to him, "Follow me".

Peter turned and saw following them the disciple whom Jesus loved, who had lain close to his breast at the supper and had said, "Lord, who is it that is going to betray you?" When Peter saw him, he said to Jesus, "Lord what about this man?" Jesus said to him, "If it is my will that he remain until I come, what is that to you? Follow me!" The saying spread abroad among the brethren that this disciple was not to die; yet Jesus did not say to him that he was not to die, but "If it is my will that he remain until I come, what is that to you".

This is the disciple who is bearing witness to these things, and who has written these things; and we know that his testimony is true.

But there are also many other things which Jesus did; were every one of them to be written, I suppose that the world itself could not contain the books that would be written.

To begin, this chapter is obviously an appendix to the Gospel. How it got there has been a matter of intense scholarly interest and debate. I have an explanation, which makes sense if the author is Judas-Beloved Disciple, and which will be detailed later. But for the present let us test the assumption that this later chapter was written by Judas–Beloved Disciple and added at a later date for reasons to be explained.

In this chapter Jesus appears to the disciples by the Sea of Tiberias. This, then, is one of only two (the other, Matthew Chapter 16 to end) resurrection appearances that took place outside Jerusalem or environs (not counting the reference in Mark 16:7).

The Beloved Disciple is not named in the list of those disciples who were together and who went fishing on Peter's initiative (21:1-3).[10] Why? He could

---

[10] Martin Hengel (p. 16 ff) refers to the similarity between the lists of the disciples in Papias and John 1 and John 21. The number of disciples in each of the three lists varies but the order is strikingly similar. Hengel draws the conclusion that Papias was dependent upon the Fourth Gospel. He gives convincing reasons for the differences between the Synoptics and the Fourth Gospel, drawing attention to the Johannine relative lack of interest in the 12 disciples, important in the Markan source, and for Papias' substitution of the disciple Matthew for Nathaniel (as in the lists given in the Fourth Gospel). He notes also the Fourth Gospel's strange reluctance to call James and John by name and to refer to them simply as the sons of Zebedee (as 21:2).

By the Sea of Tiberias "Lord, what about this man?"
John 21:20-22. Peter turned and saw following them the disciple whom Jesus loved, who had lain close to his breast at the supper and had said, "Lord, who is it that is going to betray you?" When Peter saw him, he said to Jesus, "Lord, what about this man?" Jesus said to him, "If it is my will that he remain until I come, what is that to you? Follow me!"

have been one of the "two others" (unnamed, verse 1) but if so, why not name him? We would doubt, in view of the author's known precision in names that this is simply an omission. One explanation is that Judas–Beloved Disciple had "come along" but was beginning to be ostracized from the apostolic band. He was there, but not with them. By this time the apostles had realized the import and enormity of the betrayal. Things were mixed up and confused. There were no heroes. Peter had denied the Lord, the rest of the apostles had fled, Judas had betrayed him. But the Lord had entrusted him to his mother, and Mary may have made a plea for her adopted son. Judas himself didn't know where he stood. He felt the power of Jesus' forgiveness from the cross, but he also felt the power of the apostles' enmity. He didn't feel welcome in the Upper Room, but he followed along to Galilee. So he was there, he was ashamed of himself, he

(E) Catalogues of Twelve Disciples in Ancient Sources

Papias (7 + 2)	Andrew	Peter	Philip	Thomas	James	John	Matthew	Aristion	Presbyter John	(two not of the Twelve)
John 1 (1 + 4) (one unknown)	Andrew	Peter	Philip		Nathanael					
John 21 (5 + 2)	Peter		Thomas	Nathanael			Sons of Zebedee		two unknown disciples	
Philip of Side (4 + 2)	Peter	John	Philip	Thomas				Aristion	Presbyter John	
Mark 3 (12)	Peter	James	John	Andrew	Philip	Bartholomew	Matthew	Thomas		
Acts 1 (11)	Peter	John	James	Andrew	Philip	Thomas	Bartholomew	Matthew		
Epistula Apostolorum (11)	John	Thomas	Peter	Andrew	James	Philip	Bartholomew	Matthew	Nathanael	
Apostolic Constitutions (12)	John	Matthew	Peter	Andrew	Philip	James	Nathanael	Thomas	Cephas	Bartholomew

Taken from Hengel, The Johannine Question.

wanted to be with them, but could not. This may be expressed in a very poignant way in the fact that he wasn't with them when Peter suggested fishing. We can see him, lingering on the fringes or trailing along behind. We note Peter appears to be still the leader, it was he who made the suggestion that the band go fishing. This explanation seems fanciful and unnecessary.

Another explanation for not naming the Beloved Disciple as present in the group would be to preserve the anonymity of the author while being as precise as possible about who actually was there.

Hengel states without equivocation that "Another analogy is provided by the two 'disciples of the Lord' who do not belong to the Twelve at the end of the Papias list and the *two unknown disciples in John 21:2 who preserve the incognito of the beloved disciple*".

Thus, if he had named all the disciples except Judas (i.e. leaving one unidentified disciple) then the identity of the Beloved Disciple could be deduced not only by those who had been there (who could probably have guessed anyway) but also by any who had heard the story. What the author or redactor of the Fourth Gospel was concerned with here (and had to protect himself against) was the existence of oral or written material which had not come to his attention. *By leaving two unidentified disciples it made it impossible to identify the Beloved Disciple with any certainty with either of the disciples described as "other" but who were known to be there (from other sources).* Another possibility was to name all the disciples present, including Judas, refer to the "Beloved Disciple" where he does (in the boat) and leave it to the reader to guess which he is. But this would have been a trick on the reader (and an unnecessary one) and would have given the Christian world one piece of information which was unnecessary (i.e. that Judas was there) and dangerous because it would have contradicted Matthew and Luke-Acts account of Judas' death, thus calling into conflict the credulity of the Fourth Gospel. It was better to leave him dead to protect the source of the Gospel. It was also better not to give away any further information to those who might not have it and who might use it to guess the identity of the author.

In any case he was there, out in the boat, when the figure appeared on the beach. And it was the Beloved Disciple who first realized that it was Jesus as well as the first to believe in the significance of the empty tomb, first here to recognize Our Lord on the beach. Once again the Beloved Disciple and Peter act in concert. The Beloved Disciple addresses his discovery to Peter ("It is the Lord!" 21:7).

This time, unlike the empty tomb, it is Peter who gets there first. While they eat breakfast on the beach, the Beloved Disciple–Judas recedes into the background, once again unsure of his position.

Then comes Peter's catechism by Jesus. 21:15-19. If we ask the question,

"Why did Judas choose the particular pseudonym, 'Beloved Disciple'" we find an answer in this passage. Peter's catechism would not be of particular concern to this study except for one interesting fact. In the catechism there is the curious and much probed mystery of the use of two Greek words for "love" ($\phi\iota\lambda\epsilon\omega$ and $\dot{\alpha}\gamma\alpha\pi\dot{\alpha}\omega$)[11]. It is the conclusion of most commentators that John uses these more or less interchangeably (Westcott being a notable exception). So the use of the two Greek words likewise in describing "Beloved Disciple" is not to be considered significant. But, taking the two together, was the author Beloved Disciple–Judas in his use of these two Greek words for love trying to establish the association between himself and Peter? This may lie behind his very use of the pseudonym the "Beloved"? Is he saying, by choosing this name, and by mixing the Greek in both cases, in effect, "Peter and I were together as followers of Jesus and close friends. We were associates and, together, leaders in the apostolic band. What Jesus said to Peter applied in a sense to me. I, too, was loved by Jesus. If I hadn't stumbled so badly perhaps that catechism would have been mine". Or (an alternative theory) he chose the pseudonym, Beloved Disciple, to remind Peter of Judas' special status, either to thank Peter anonymously and, posthumously for his protection and pastoral care of Judas in the period following the betrayal (if Peter had protected him) or to recall Peter's responsibilities as emphasized in this critical meeting with the risen Lord (if Peter had turned against him).[12]

Now comes a critical point. In 21:20, after the catechism, "Peter turned and saw following them the disciple whom Jesus loved". The Beloved Disciple is trailing along behind and on the fringe. The text continues, "Who had lain close to his breast at the supper and said, "Lord, who is it that is going to betray you?" (21:20). Here the author takes pains to ensure the reader connects this Beloved Disciple with the one in the Upper Room.

When Peter saw him he said to Jesus, "Lord, what about this man?"

Why should there be a question about this man? Westcott[13] finds this "a perfectly natural question". Is it really? Peter has just been told that he will die a

---

[11] Bernard ICC vol. 2, page 702ff has a convenient summary of the ways and places in which the two Greek words are used and in John.

[12] This makes two assumptions (1) that Chapter 21 was written by the Beloved Disciple but added later by the redactor; (2) "publication of the whole of the Gospel was delayed until Peter and the relatively few others who could make the positive identification of Beloved Disciple with Judas were dead or could be counted upon to keep quiet (e.g. John the Apostle)". This will be referred to later.

[13] Westcott, page 305.

By the Sea of Tiberias "Lord, what about this man?"

John 21:20-22. Peter turned and saw following them the disciple whom Jesus loved, who had lain close to his breast at the supper and had said, "Lord, who is it that is going to betray you?" When Peter saw him, he said to Jesus, "Lord, what about this man?" Jesus said to him, "If it is my will that he remain until I come, what is that to you? Follow me!"

martyr's death (21:18).[14] So the question might be taken in the sense that, "I know *my* fate, what about my mate". But that could equally have been asked of any of the others. Another possibility is that Peter has just been given a commission to "Feed my sheep". The Beloved Disciple has featured prominently in the Fourth Gospel. He has been associated closely with Peter. What is his role in the Church, for the future? Neither of these possibilities seem

---

[14] Although the authenticity of this prediction has been challenged. Brown, page 1107, says this "Tho language is very vague, for example Schlatter, page 371, holds that the outstretched arms refers to the position assumed in prayer; and many think that a more general statement about Peter's future has subsequently and post eventum been applied to Peter's death (vs. 19)". If this is true, then it would support my belief that the Gospel had to be delayed from general circulation until Peter's death and this was the work of an editor.

satisfactory. For Jesus' answer seems to assume that there is something else involved in the question. Jesus does not speak about roles in the Church, or assign the Beloved Disciple any special role. Jesus said to him, "If it is my will that he remain until I come, what is that to you? Follow me!" Brown,[15,16] has this to say about the Greek text:

"'to remain', the verb *menein* can mean 'to stay alive' as in I Cor. 15:6, and that is the idea here";

"'until I come' even without the evidence of vs. 21, this is scarcely a reference to Jesus' coming in death, for every Christian must remain until Jesus visits him in death. Though Marrow suggests the possibility of hyperbole ("Suppose I want this disciple to live forever"), most commentators find in this saying an expectation that Jesus' second coming would happen within a short time after the resurrection". (Brown also mentions that for Westcott the coming is "a slow and continuous realization").

"'how does that concern you? Literally "what to you?"'; this expression *ti pros* with a pronoun is classical (BDF, 127) and is akin to the expression used in 2.4 (which lacked the *pros*). It is also used in Matt. 27.4 where, after Judas accused himself of guilt in betraying Jesus, the high priests respond, 'what is that to us?'"

"'Your concern to follow me;' literally 'You follow me', In the similar command in 19 the Greek pronoun 'you' is not used, so that its appearance here is emphatic, by contrasting Peter with the Beloved

---

[15] Brown, page 1109.

[16] Bultmann's analysis of this chapter is outlandish (page 702). "The information in v. 9, that when they come to the shore they find a coal fire there, on which fish was roasting, and bread as well, is surprising after v.5, in consequence of which the disciples were sent out for a catch to procure provisions which were not at hand." (A real possibility is that they were not just going fishing to provide a meal for themselves. They had been professional fishermen, they were fishing for food for their families, or for sale.) "Should a miracle be reported that make the fish caught by the disciples superfluous, and that shows human effort to be unnecessary in face of the omnipotence of the 'Lord' who can miraculously provide what is lacking? But the catch of fish itself was a miracle, due to his omnipotence." (Jesus started the meal, and even if we are concerned here with what was eaten, he could have made his own contribution, started cooking, and been prepared to add theirs when they arrived. The catch need not have been miraculous. Some commentators have suggested Jesus was simply a good fisherman who, by his observance of natural phenomena, and his experience on the lake, knew where to cast the net. Or did he see a shoal, as another commentator suggests.) "Moreover in v.10 Jesus again speaks from the standport of v.5; the disciples must bring in their catch! For what reason, if not to prepare a meal with the fish that have just been caught?" (Yes it is conceivable that he wanted them to bring in their catch. They might have been inclined to leave it there in their excitement.) "And in v.11 Peter – manifestly at the command of Jesus – disembarks onto the ▶

Disciple who will not follow Jesus to death in the same way that Peter will follow". (But I, say that the contrast is other than that.)

In addition Bernard[17] has this to say:

"on vs. 22 "If it is my will (θέλω is here the θέλω of masterful authority (cf. 7.24) that he should tarry (μένειν is used of survival, as in I Cor. 15:6, until I come, what is that to thee? ". . . The emphasis is on ἐὰν θέλω. Jesus is not represented as saying that it is His will that the Beloved Disciple would survive; but that if it was His will, that was no concern of Peter's.

Now, if we put all this together in a closer examination of the text, the following picture emerges. Peter turned and saw following them the disciple whom Jesus loved, who had lain close to his breast at the supper and had said, "Lord, who is it that is going to betray you?" The author was probably not entirely sure that the designation "Beloved Disciple", which had been used sparingly, and which might not have been picked up by a casual reader or one who was reading this section without having read the whole; and he wanted to make doubly sure, at this important juncture, that there could be absolutely no mistaking the connection, i.e. who he was referring to. When Peter saw him, he said to Jesus, "This man, what?" (implying in the question by its simplicity that Jesus would know to what matter or concern he was referring). Jesus said to him, "If it is my (emphatic! as though you, Peter, should question my authority) will that he should stay alive (survive) until I come (2nd coming)[18], what is that to you?" It is a fine touch, or irony, if the author Beloved Disciple–Judas used, or found Jesus using, the same words (What is that to you/us?) to Peter that Matthew (27:3) reports were used to Judas by the high priests after the betrayal

---

▶   shore and draws the net with the fish in it to land! But Peter was a long while before the ship, and therefore had swum to land before the other disciples! Of course it is not expressly said in v.7 that he had arrived; but that he who wanted to get in front of the others actually arrived after them should certainly have had to be stated expressly. Accordingly he was standing there for sometime, and Jesus appears to take no notice of him, etc." (A boat can be rowed, or pulled in shallow water, as fast, or faster than a man can swim. There is no need to assume Peter was standing around for a long time. Nor is there a need for us to have a record of what Jesus said to Peter when he arrived on shore. The eyewitness was in the boat!) If Bultmann were simply giving his interpretation of the story that would be one thing (we could agree or disagree). But he gives it as proof that the story is so confused as to be unsupportable in its present form. His interpretation, in my opinion, is far more confused than the story!

[17] Bernard, page 711 vol. 2.

[18] The Greek also supports "while I come" as well as "until I come", thus Jesus could even have been referring to another resurrection appearance.

and which he would remember with acute shame the rest of his life). The author of the Fourth Gospel may not have recorded this incident because it was connected with the false account of Judas' death or because it wasn't true (but even if untrue, was useful to him).

"You (emphatic) follow me"; following me is *your* concern and if you intend to truly follow me you will accept my decision on Beloved Disciple–Judas even though you may not be able to understood or to forgive to that degree yourself. My will then becomes your will in this matter as in everything.

If this reconstruction is acceptable, and it seems a reasonable one, then we can see it having developed from the following situation. Judas–Beloved Disciple–Judas had been reluctant, afraid of his reception, no doubt, to venture into the Upper Room, but he did trail along to Galilee. The disciples didn't know exactly what to make of him, or what to do with him. We can't know how much information they had about what had happened at the scene of the betrayal, or at the Cross. But it would seem probable that they knew of Jesus' commending Mary and the Beloved Disciple, each to the other, as he hung on the cross.

They had by this time (eight days plus presumably the time it took to travel to Galilee) plenty of time to talk it all over, share experiences, and they had a good idea of the basic facts. So the problem of what to do with Judas–Beloved Disciple was a real one. The high priests didn't want him. Could the Christian community, even, forgive such a heinous crime? So the question by Peter was a very natural one. It was crying for an answer. Next to his own responsibilities, just detailed, it was the most important immediate matter to be decided. In fact, since he had just been asked if he loved the Lord, and been given pastoral oversight, Peter might well have thought it was Jesus' will that the first item on the agenda was what to do with the traitor.

To this question, Jesus, well knowing what Peter was asking, gave an emphatic answer. "If it was my will (already expressed on the cross in the sense that Jesus had commended Mary to Judas and Judas to Mary) that he should survive, why are you raising the matter again? It is not, strictly speaking, your prerogative to question this. You have said you love me. Now prove it, in following me". We can imagine the Lord's impatience that after all the ground they had covered Peter was still being thick about something as basic as forgiveness. If Jesus had forgiven him then Peter should be able to do so, and to influence the apostolic band to do so.

Continuing with the text, vs. 23 has caused speculation and debate about whether it means that the Beloved is dead at the time of writing of this chapter. It would not seem as though it can be said with any certainty whether he is or is not dead. The fact that this rumour circulated in the early Christian community is interesting. If speculation were going to be rife, it is far more likely that Beloved Disciple-Judas would have been the object of speculation than Beloved Disciple. Precisely what the rumour was that spread among the brethren is hard to ascertain. If Judas were still alive (and not dead as St. Matthew and St. Luke – in Acts – report) then the rumour could be based upon the question natural in the minds of the apostles, "Should Judas die for the crime of betrayal?" If the answer to this, perhaps based upon Mary's testimony, was that he should not die, then this answer might have been twisted to mean Judas was never to die or not to die until the second coming, and it could be this kind of misinterpretation that the author was trying to put to rest. Of course Judas–Beloved Disciple author would have had a particular interest in the subject!

The testimony as to the authorship at the end of John 21 is mentioned in the separate section on the *Internal Evidence of Authorship* (following).

(F) *The Other Disciple*

There is another place in which the Beloved Disciple might be referred to, *The High Priest's Court* 18:15-16. "Simon Peter followed Jesus, and so did the other disciple. As this disciple was known to the high priest, he entered the court of the high priest along with Jesus, while Peter stood outside at the door. So the other disciple, who was known to the high priest, went out and spoke to the maid who kept the door, and brought Peter in".

Is this other disciple the Beloved Disciple?[19]

The main reason that this "other disciple" has been identified with the Beloved Disciple is the reference in John 20:2 "So she (Mary Magdalene) ran, and went to Simon Peter and *the other disciple*, the one whom Jesus loved, etc". There is the question of why the author would have left this other disciple of 8:16 unnamed. Surely, if he knew so much about him, that he went with Peter, that he knew the high priest and that he secured Peter's entrance, he must have

---

[19] This question has been well investigated. It is worth noting that Cullman (*Peter, Disciple, Apostle, Martyr* by Oscar Cullman, page 27), assumes the "other disciple" is the Beloved Desciple. Hengel (page 125) writes, "Finally mention should be made here of the mysterious "other disciple" who gains direct access to the palace of Annas, at that time the most influential man in Jerusalem, because he was well-acquainted with him or a friend of his (18.15 f: *en gnostos to archiere*). He can therefore introduce Peter into the Palace. "We should have no doubt that the beloved disciple is meant here." Smalley (page 80), on the other hand, believes it unlikely that the "other disciple" was the "beloved disciple" but does so because his hypothesis is that the beloved disciple is John the apostle. He finds it strange to believe that John the apostle would be as familiar with the high priest's family as this passage would suggest.

also known his name! Why didn't he identify him? Once again, if we assume a scrupulous writer, and the author is particularly exact in identifying people, then we should assume a purpose in concealment. First of all, if we grant the responsible nature of the author, it follows that he meant to imply by the wording of 20:2 to the careful reader that this was the Beloved Disciple. Why did he not say so? If the author were Judas–Beloved Disciple he had four options here. They were: (1) to leave this section (18:15-16) out entirely. But there is important information here, and it gives credence to Peter's denial which, in turn is an important key to his character and basic to the deep import of Jesus' commission to Peter in 21:15-19 (Peter entrusted even after his denial). Peter's role is an important and well detailed part of the Gospel. It was important to the author to establish his credentials here as an eyewitness. Having decided to leave it in, he could.

(2) Use the name, "Beloved Disciple". But, if my theory is correct, he needed to conceal the fact that the Beloved Disciple was Judas in order to have his Gospel accepted for what it was. So (and this will be developed further in the summary to this section) he selected occasions to use the Beloved Disciple designation when he was certain that those present were dead or where their silence could be counted on. This was not one of those places. There were many people around, presumably some of them young (e.g. the servant girl) who might still be alive and could identify the Beloved Disciple as Judas.

(3) Use the name, Judas. I don't know why he didn't unless he thought that the detail of the account of Peter's denial might be suspect if it were seen as coming from the man who had so recently betrayed his Lord. Wherever Judas appears in the Gospel elsewhere there are others around who could have provided the information. Perhaps he wanted to establish some link with the Beloved Disciple (and the claims made for authenticity in Chapter 20.30 and 21:24-25) but not nail it down too tightly.

(4) Leave the disciple unnamed. This is what he did, but established a suitably tenuous link.

To summarize, there are reasons to believe, in addition to those previously advanced by commentators, and in accord with the general premise of this study, that the "other disciple" of 18:15-16 is the Beloved Disciple. Cullman and Hengel argue that he is. In addition, if this were true, and if the Judas is the Beloved Disciple–author it explains very readily how that "other disciple" had ready access to the high priests, knowing or having enough authority on the premises to tell the maid to let Peter in.

It points to a closer relationship of Judas to the high priestly household than we have reason to believe otherwise. The maid's question can be seen as not just idle curiosity. With Jesus being questioned on the premises it is highly likely that the household (maid included) was instructed to be alert and to report on any followers of Jesus who might appear. The fact that the "other disciple" was able on his own authority to gain access for Peter and has easy movement for himself shows a considerable acquaintance with and influence in the inner circle of the Jewish hierarchy. This is not to be entirely explained on the basis that he had betrayed Jesus. Traitors are not usually considered, even by those who benefit, as reliable people.

(G) *The Unnamed Disciple*

1:35-42 and 19:34-37. There are two other places where it has been suggested the Beloved Disciple may be involved, although not identified as such.

The first of these is 1:35-42.

> The next day again John was standing with two of his disciples; and he looked at Jesus as he walked, and said, "Behold, the Lamb of God!" The two disciples heard him say this, and they followed Jesus. Jesus turned, and saw them following, and said to them, "What do you seek?" And they said to him, "Rabbi (which means Teacher), where are you staying?" He said to them, "Come and see". They came and saw where he was staying; and they stayed with him that day, for it was about the tenth hour. One of the two who heard John speak, and followed him, was Andrew, Simon Peter's brother. He first found his brother Simon, and said to him, "We have found the Messiah" (which means Christ). He bought him to Jesus. Jesus looked at him and said, "So you are Simon the son of John? You shall be called Cephas" (which means Peter).

Here two of John the Baptist's disciples follow Jesus and become followers of Jesus. One of these is named as Andrew, Simon Peter's brother. The other is left unnamed. Why? The obvious answer is that the author or source didn't have this information. Another answer is that the author wanted to leave a trace of himself (as may be the case in Mark 14:51) in the strange incident where a young man fled naked after witnessing Jesus' betrayal by Judas). In any case this incident (1:35-42) doesn't shed much light on the authorship of the Gospel or identity of the Beloved Disciple.

The second place where it has been suggested the Beloved Disciple might be referred to is 19:34-37. "But one of the soldiers pierced his side with a spear, and at once there came out blood and water. He who saw it has borne witness – his testimony is true, and he knows that he tells the truth – that you also may believe. For these things took place that the scripture might be fulfilled, "Not a bone of him shall be broken". And again another scripture says, "They shall look on him whom they have pierced". Here the author or source deemed it necessary to claim eyewitness authority for the account that water and blood came out of Jesus' side when he was pierced by the soldier's sword. Since the author is claiming the authority of "bearing witness" (21:24) for the whole of the Gospel it seems odd that he should make particular reference to the fact that he has "borne witness" at this point. Once again it doesn't appear significant to the identity of the Beloved Disciple.

(H) *Summary of Chapter II*

There are several general conclusions which can be drawn from the analysis of the places where the Beloved Disciple appears in the Fourth Gospel.

(1) *The Beloved Disciple appears at critical points in the Gospel.* If one of us were to have the opportunity to choose four times when we might have been present during Our Lord's ministry, we might very well choose the Upper Room, the foot of the Cross, the Empty Tomb and a Resurrection scene (particularly the one by the Sea of Tiberias at daybreak). The reason we would choose these is that they were critical points in Our Lord's ministry. This is one reason they were chosen by the author of the Fourth Gospel. Of paramount importance to him was the preservation and conveyance of the Gospel that he, and he alone, could give to the Church. He must establish the credentials of the author. The way to establish these credentials was to establish the fact that the account was from an eyewitness, and that this eyewitness was present at critical points in Our Lord's ministry. This is the reason why the name Beloved Disciple is used at these four places.

At the same time he must preserve his anonymity. The other, equally important reason in the case of the Upper Room is that, if Judas were named as being the recipient of the conversation with Jesus then the source of this account (Judas) and, inferentially, of the whole of the Gospel would be manifest as Judas himself.

The reference in 18:15-16 (if it is to the Beloved Disciple) is explained for different reasons (as above).

(2) *The designation Beloved Disciple was necessary at the points used to preserve the author's anonymity.* It was vital to ensure that the author could not be certainly identified as Judas because the Church might well have rejected it out of hand as being the unreliable work of the disciple who betrayed their Lord. Thus the term Beloved Disciple was chosen to disguise who the eyewitness was. No one, especially those in close touch with eyewitness accounts or early sources

must be able to identify or to demonstrate from their own experience that the Beloved Disciple was Judas. This was done by carefully and skillfully choosing incidents in which there were few people present, where the fate of these people was known (or their silence could be counted on), and where it was highly desirable to acknowledge an eyewitness account while it was essential to preserve anonymity. Thus, in two of the incidents (the Cross and the Empty Tomb) there was a relatively small group involved, whose whereabouts and deaths would most likely have been known. In the other two incidents (the Upper Room and the Sea of Tiberias) the apostles were present, but once more their deaths would have been reported in the early Christian Church. Thus, in the Upper Room incident, it is probable that one of the other disciples might just have remembered who it was of whom Peter asked the question.

(3) This (2) above accounts partially for the delay in circulating the Fourth Gospel. The author had to wait until those in the inner circle who would know from their own personal participation in the events described that Judas was the disciple designated as Beloved Disciple. Thus the promulgation of the Fourth Gospel had to be delayed until the disciples themselves and participants had died. This, in turn, accounts in part for the oft remarked dichotomy between the marks of eyewitness accounts and the late date assigned by most scholars to the Fourth Gospel.

(4) *The name "Beloved Disciple" was substituted for "Judas" after the betrayal because the use of "Judas" itself would have caused difficulties.* In particular, if Judas has been identified as present at the Sea of Tiberias (when Matthew and Acts had him dead), then the credibility of the Fourth Gospel on this point (and weakening the case for the whole) would have been called into question. Also, to have Judas as prominent as he would have been in the latter stages (cross and empty tomb) when many in the Church apparently didn't know this from the synoptic tradition and might not want to be told it, would, again, have caused unnecessary conflict with the synoptic tradition and therefore difficulties of a kind the author did not want.

(5) *The name, Beloved Disciple, was chosen with care because it established the "spiritual credentials" of the author.* Not only was he there, but he was a man the Lord loved. This kind of information is important.

On the other hand, it wasn't a designation used by Jesus or one which pointed firmly to any of the twelve disciples. In a real sense Jesus loved all the disciples. Those who might have known of a special relationship between Judas and Jesus (the other eleven) had died by the time the Fourth Gospel became generally known.

If a man is writing about events in Uganda in 1981 we want to know about him. Is he black or white, is he Ugandan, if so a member of which tribe and was he associated with Amin's regime? What is his political orientation? Is he Christian or Moslem, Roman Catholic or Anglican, etc? Is he a westerner, if so French, British, American, Russian? If journalism or history could be really written objectively such information would have no relevance. Since it cannot be (and in the writing of secular history this has been recognised) it is pertinent to know these facts. Now the author of the Fourth Gospel[20] couldn't tell us very much, because of his special problem, but he told us enough; that he was a (the) disciple the Lord loved. This was true and of the highest relevance. We know that he was there in the bosom of the Lord.

(6) It is interesting to note the close association shown in the Fourth Gospel between Peter and the Beloved Disciple; between (less obvious and less certain) Mary Magdalene and the Beloved Disciple. Peter appears with the Beloved Disciple in three out of four of the incidents in which the Beloved Disciple appears (four out of five if 18:15-16 is accepted as a Beloved Disciple incident). Mary Magdalene appears in two of the four (or five). In one of these the three appear together (i.e. the Empty Tomb) and this is especially significant since Mary apparently may have gone to two places to inform these two. Was there some special relationship between the three? We cannot say for certain, but it seems probable.

Also, the author didn't write down in the Gospel everything he knew (21:25). He made a selection. Was that selection partly dictated by the fact that he could count on Peter's silence? The reason that he could count on it may have been because of personal friendship. But more likely it was that in the Gospel incidents that circulated in the early Church it became obvious that Peter had not mentioned him in the incidents in which the Beloved Disciple appears. Or, even, more likely, if Mark's Gospel is based in part upon Peter's recollections then the author of the Fourth Gospel waited until he saw what Peter (in Mark) had said (and also Matthew and Luke) so that he knew what was recorded and therefore what could be presumed known by the Church at large. This was another reason for delaying release of the Fourth Gospel.

(7) The close association of the Beloved Disciple and Peter has been noted. In the Upper Room, Peter and the Beloved Disciple were the two named disciples, and Peter asked the Beloved Disciple to query who was to betray Jesus. The Fourth Gospel does not mention Peter at the Cross, the second time the

---

[20] To be sure the Synoptic authors didn't give us biographical information. It would have been nice if they had. But even so, it is a different approach, perhaps necessitated by the fact that no one man exercised the same editorial control over the whole as the author of the Fourth Gospel.

Beloved Disciple designation is used. At the Empty Tomb it is Peter and the Beloved Disciple whom Mary notifies first and they run together. The possible connection of Mary Magdalene and the Beloved Disciple/Judas has already been noted (page 59 above). Peter and Beloved Disciple were closely connected in the resurrection appearance by the Sea of Tiberias (21). If the "other disciple" of 18:15-16 is the Beloved Disciple (see page 54 above, especially footnote, page 55) then here, too, there is a close relationship between Peter and the Beloved Disciple. So in three out of four, or four out of five (if 18:15-16 is included) of the incidents in which the Beloved Disciple designation is used, there is a close connection between Peter and the Beloved Disciple.

(8) Cullman in his book on Peter comments on the close relationship in the Fourth Gospel between Peter and the Beloved Disciple. Although his primary concern is to show this affected Peter's position in the circle of disciples, he says this,

"A somewhat different picture emerges when we turn to the Gospel of John. Here the outstanding role of Peter, which is unchallenged in the Synoptic Gospels, becomes a problem, since for this Evangelist the mysterious unnamed "Beloved Disciple" of Jesus enters into a certain competition with Peter. Thus here, in a way different from the Synoptics, a contemporary interest in the author concerning the position of Peter may have influenced the presentation. However, it is noteworthy that this Gospel, which manifestly wishes to emphasize the particularly close relationship between Jesus and the "Beloved Disciple" nevertheless nowhere attempts to deny the special role of Peter within the group of disciples."[21]

---

[21] Cullman, "Peter," page 27.

Chapter III

Fourth Gospel References
to Judas Iscariot

In this section we set the stage into our investigation by considering the references to Judas by the author of the Fourth Gospel and the possible significance of these.

The principle references to Iscariot by name, or references to him as traitor, may be grouped in five incidents. They are:

(A) Betrayal Forecast (6:70-71);
(B) The Anointing by Mary (12:1-8);
(C) The Upper Room (13);
(D) The High Priestly Prayer (17:12);
(E) Gethsemane (18:2-12)

(A) *Betrayal Forecast* 6:70-71

> Jesus answered them, "Did I not choose you, the twelve, and one of you is a devil?" He spoke of Judas the son of Simon Iscariot, for he, one of the twelve, was to betray him.

This incident followed the feeding of the 5,000 in John's Gospel. Jesus' teaching about the feeding was detailed, was astounding and disturbing to the disciples. "I am the bread of life; he who comes to me shall not hunger, and he who believes in me shall never thirst" 6:35. Further (6:51) Jesus went on to say "I am the living bread which came down from heaven; if anyone eats of this bread he will live forever; and the bread which I shall give for the life of the world is my flesh". Even if one argues that the latter has such strong Eucharistic connotations that its location this early in the Gospel is suspect, nonetheless the claims made by Jesus in this chapter are so wide ranging as to cause sceptism and a falling away. "After this *many* of his disciples drew back and no longer went about with him" (John 6:66). The twelve stayed with him. Jesus (answered

---

1. The word translated "devil" is used here and in John 8.44 and 13.2, always to mean one inspired by Satan.

them), "Did I not choose you, the twelve, and one of you is a devil?"[1] He spoke of Judas the son of Simon Iscariot,[2] for he, one of the twelve, was to betray him. (John 6:70-71). The author of the Gospel here displays a knowledge of what was in Jesus' mind. How did he know? The simple answer is that it was a deduction made from the knowledge of the betrayal later acquired (hindsight is easier than foresight). Another possible answer is that it is consistent with the author's special concern to show that Jesus was in full knowledge of events and people (see John 6:6, 13:1 etc.). But another possible answer is that Judas (that is if he were the author) had a clue of Jesus' demeanour other than non-verbal indications in that Jesus knew at this point that he (Judas) was to be the betrayer. In the light of what follows (that is each case where Judas is mentioned in the Gospel, the author had a special knowledge applicable to Judas), I would choose a combination of the last two reasons, and the following is a reasonable reconstruction in summary. Jesus fed the 5,000. He made certain astounding claims based upon this. Many of those who had followed him were disturbed. Perhaps they hadn't heard or fully assimilated what had gone before (e.g. the claims made at Jacob's well). The claim to be more important than Moses was bound to upset the Jews. For many this was the watershed. They had followed so far, attracted by his teaching and personality, but could go no further. Judas was not one of these, but this is where he first began to have doubts. Remembering this, and remembering that Jesus had here spoken for the first time to the twelve about a betrayer, and believing that Jesus had full knowledge, including detailed foreknowledge, he believed that Jesus knew at this time that he was to betray him

(B) *Anointing by Mary* 12:1-8[3]

> Six days before the Passover, Jesus came to Bethany, where Lazarus was, whom Jesus had raised from the dead. There they made him a supper; Martha served, but Lazarus was one of those at table with him. Mary took a pound of costly ointment of pure nard and anointed the feet of Jesus and wiped his feet with her hair; and the house was filled with the fragrance of

---

[2] There are several explanations for the name Iscariot. The most probable is that it meant Man of Kerioth. There are two Kerioths in the Old Testament, in Moab and in Judah. In either case, it wasn't Galilee, and Judas can be assumed to be the only non-Galilean of the twelve.

[3] This is an involved exegetical problem in relating the Fourth Gospel account to those in the Synoptics (Mark 14:3-9, Matthew 26:6-13, Luke 7:36-50). Was there more than one incident? Were there two women or one? None of this seems to affect the substance of what follows. There is a good summary of the evidence in the ICC Commentary of St. John by J. H. Bernard.

the ointment. But Judas Iscariot, one of his disciples (he who was to betray him) said, "Why was this ointment not sold for three hundred denarii and given to the poor?" This he said, not that he cared for the poor but because he was a thief, and as he had the money box he used to take what was put into it. Jesus said, "Let her alone, let her keep it for the day of my burial. The poor you always have with you, but you do not always have me".

Here Judas objects to the fact that Mary has used a costly ointment to anoint Jesus' feet. He thinks that the money might have been better used. But Judas Iscariot, one of his disciples (he who was to betray him) said, "Why was this ointment not sold for three hundred denarii and given to the poor? This he said, *not that he cared for the poor* but because he was a thief, and as he had the money box he used to take what was put into it". John 12:4-6. How did the author know that Judas didn't care for the poor, was concerned because of self interest? One answer could be that the author found out later (if the disciples had known at the time Judas would not have been allowed to continue as Treasurer) that Judas had been a thief and, in the light of the betrayal, and in the all too human desire to blacken a known villain, added his deduction that Judas was not sincere in his concern. The other explanation is that the author had good reason to know what was in Judas' mind. The first explanation assumes that the author[4] deliberately made a statement of doubtful accuracy, based upon deduction to take a gratuitous slap at Judas. The second explanation seems reasonable. Judas, the author, knew Judas, the Treasurer, was a thief. He was honest or disingenuous enough to mention it.

---

[4] Of course, there is always the possibility that the dishonesty was not the author's but in the material he had at his disposal, but that doesn't affect the basic argument.

(C) *Upper Room* John 13

The Upper Room must be the scene most depicted by artists of all ages of all types, using canvas, wood, stone, plaster, etc. When an artist attempts to depict a scene he or she needs to sort through all manner of interpretive and theological issues. These are seen in body languages, facial expressions and a multitude of other small details. Of particular interest in this study are depictions of the Upper Room as described in John 13. Three groups of photos follow:

Victorian reredos at the Parish Church of St. John the Evangelist, Cheetham, Diocese of Manchester.

We are fortunate to have the Architect's sketch and letter describing this work.

The entire reredos.

Jesus giving the sop and holding a bowl.

Another close-up showing the group on Jesus' right.

Another close-up – note facial expressions and body language.

Architect's sketch.

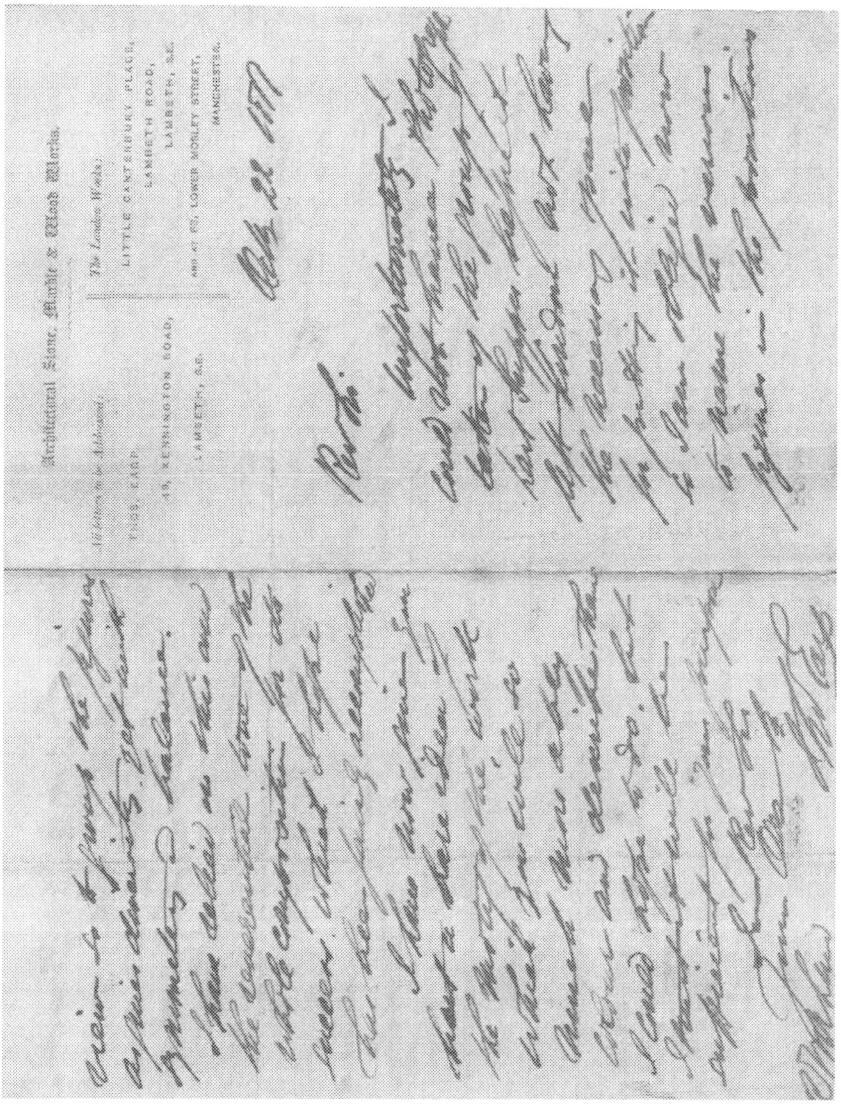

Architectural Stone, Marble & Mosaic Works.

The London Works:

LITTLE CANTERBURY PLACE,
LAMBETH ROAD,
LAMBETH, S.E.

AND AT 60, LOWER MOSLEY STREET,
MANCHESTER.

Address to Address:

THOS. EARP.

48, KENNINGTON ROAD,
LAMBETH, S.E.

[handwritten letter, largely illegible]

Architect's letter.

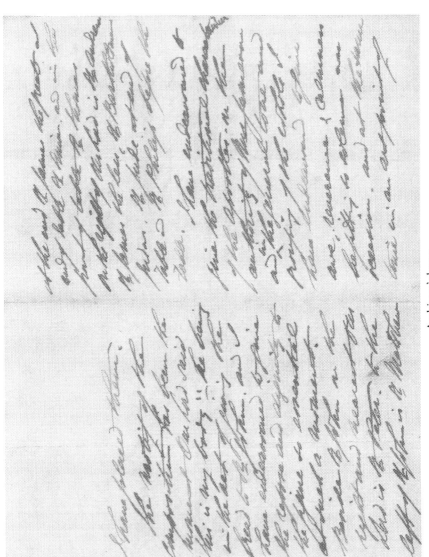

Architect's letter.

Victorian stained glass window in Smithills Hall Chapel, Smithills Dean Road,
Parish of St. Peter's, Bolton, Diocese of Manchester.

The Victorian stained glass window.

A close-up of the right centre panel of Smithills' stained glass window showing Judas with a money bag and without a halo.

(C) *Upper Room* John 13

The impending treachery of Judas permeates the Johannine account of the initial events of the Last Supper. It is referred to in 13:2, 13:11 and 13:18.

First let us look at John 13:2 "And during the supper, when the devil had already put it into the heart of Judas Iscariot, Simon's son, to betray him, Jesus . . . rose from supper, laid aside his garments, and girded himself with a towel".

This incident is interesting for three reasons. First, there is the knowledge that "the devil had already put it into the heart of Judas". Where does this information come from? There is only one who could say this with certainty.

It could be inferred from subsequent events by even a detached redactor who, knowing that Judas betrayed Jesus, reasoned that Satan entered his heart before the Last Supper because Jesus told the disciples during the Last Supper that he was to be betrayed by one of them. But why add a gratuitous bit of information based (as it had to be) only on intuition? Were there not many more important matters for consideration at this time? Second, it is curious that the author begins his narrative of the events of the Last Supper with a reference to the betrayal. Thirdly, as elsewhere, the author identifies Judas as Simon's son. This fits in with his evident determination to make certain there is no mistake in identifying Judas Iscariot as the betrayer.

Next let us look at John 13:11. After washing the disciples' feet, Jesus concludes, 13:10-11, "He who has bathed does not need to wash, except for his feet, but he is clean all over, and you are clean, but not every one of you. For he knew who was to betray him; that was why he said, 'you are not all clean'".

This is interesting for two reasons. First, there is a certain poignancy about Jesus washing Judas' feet when he knew Judas was to betray him. Presumably he did or it would have been remarked upon especially since Peter has made such a fuss about not having his feet washed. But was there only the poignancy? Did Jesus, in fact, still hope that Judas would reject Satan, not for Jesus' sake because the crucifixion was going to happen regardless of which human agents took particular roles, but for Judas' own sake? Did Jesus hope that Judas would accept the washing even as he was saying that one was not clean. Was this an attempt to bring Judas to his senses? For those who believe such matters are preordained there is no problem here. They would contend that there was no possibility of Judas changing his mind. But surely the whole thrust of Jesus' dealings with people rests upon the assurance that human beings do have a choice, can change, and can we believe that Jesus denied this to Judas even at this point?

Second, this incident is interesting because it shows a knowledge of what was in Jesus' mind. This fits in with the author's assumption at other times that he knew what was in Jesus' mind, as a beloved disciple, perhaps more than the others, might know. It is certainly true that Judas would have been more attuned to Jesus' demeanour and its meaning at this time and for this reason than any other. He knew he was going to betray Jesus, and he must have been hypersensitive about Jesus' knowledge of it.

The remarkable incident recorded in 13:21-30 needs detailed consideration. When Jesus had thus spoken, he was troubled in spirit, and testified, "Truly, truly, I say to you, one of you will betray me". The disciples looked at one another, uncertain of whom he spoke. One of his disciples, who Jesus loved, was lying close to the breast of Jesus; so Simon Peter beckoned to him and said, "Tell us who it is of whom he speaks". So lying thus, close to the breast of Jesus, he said to him, "Lord, who is it?" Jesus answered, "It is he to whom I shall give this morsel when I have dipped it". So when he had dipped the morsel, he gave it to Judas, the son of Simon Iscariot. Then after the morsel, Satan entered into him. Jesus said to him, "What you are going to do, do quickly". Now no one at the table knew why he said this to him. Some thought that, because Judas had the money box, Jesus was telling him, "Buy what we need for the feast"; or, that he should give something to the poor. So, after receiving the morsel, he immediately went out; and it was night. $\tilde{\eta}\nu$ δε νύξ "It was night" – The saddest words in the Gospel.

St. Mark (Mark 14:10-11) tells us that Judas made his compact with the Chief Priests immediately after the anointing (B, above). Thus the treachery may have been well advanced at this time. William Temple[5] surmises that the two disciples who were to prepare for the Last Supper were given a kind of cipher (St. Mark 14:13-36). Judas must not hear the description of the place so that he could alert the temple guard and thus carry out the arrest in convenient secrecy. That sacred time in the Upper Room must be kept free from interruption. This was the reason that the two disciples were told to follow the man with the pitcher of water.

I prefer Edersheim's construction of the arrangements for the Last Supper.

At the meal, Edersheim[6] believes that Jesus and his disciples reclined on their left elbows on a divan around a low eastern table. The place of honour was on Jesus' right. We can suppose something like the following[6] (minus "Judas" in place of honour at right hand side.) St. Peter is assigned the lower place (Temple) under the supposition that he went there in a fit of self-abasement

[5] William Temple, *Readings in St. John's Gospel*, page 217.
[6] *The Life and Times of Jesus the Messiah*, Edersheim, volume 2, page 494.

after the foot washing. Or he could have had the place of honour at Jesus' left. In any case it isn't central to the argument. Barclay comes to the same conclusion.[7]

This sets the scene. Jesus, we are told, was "troubled in spirit". John 13:21. Treachery by friends is more difficult to accept than opposition from enemies. Even the trial and crucifixion could not trouble him the way Judas' impending treachery, Peter's denial and the disciples falling away could. And so once again Jesus mentioned the betrayal. Was he trying to prevent it even then? We can recall his parable about the 99 sheep and the one lost sheep (Luke 15:1-10). Was he, even then, going after the "lost sheep"? It was not his way to avoid unpleasant facts. He met situations head on. The disciples probably would have preferred to ignore this unpleasantness. But this was the fourth time he had referred to it. They must ask him. It fell to Simon Peter to do so. But even here Peter used an indirect approach, to the Beloved Disciple. The Beloved Disciple asked Jesus. And here we have a procedure which lies at the crux of the matter. Commentators have assumed that Jesus' answer was spoken to the Beloved Disciple alone because it is inconceivable that it was spoken so that all could hear it. There were two swords in the room. Jesus could not have been certain that the disciples would not have taken action to restrain Judas.[8] No doubt he could have stopped them, as he did Peter later on (John 18:11) More importantly, if Jesus had made his knowledge of Judas' betrayal public then he would have, effectively, made the final decision for Judas. Jesus can be seen as not wanting to apply external pressure to prevent Judas' betrayal.

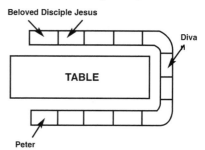

Again, Jesus might still have had hopes that Judas would resist that devil inside him. In any case, the crucifixion was inevitable and did not depend on Judas' treachery. So the answer was given to the Beloved Disciple. Lying as he was, near to the Lord's breast, the Beloved Disciple could be communicated with confidentially. But, if that is all there was to it, what is the point of answering at all? Why burden the Beloved Disciple as such with this terrible knowledge and at the same time conceal it from the others? Could Jesus have secured or depended upon the Beloved Disciple's silence? There was nothing the Beloved Disciple could *do* about it, nothing he should do about it. Judas'

[7.] Barclay, *The Master's Man.* page 69.

[8] William Barclay, *The Master's Men*, page 69. "If they had known he would never have been permitted to leave that room alive".

decision was to be his own. Jesus had decided on that long before. It is essential to his relationship with men to let them make their own choice. *BUT if Judas is the Beloved Disciple then the whole matter becomes logical and highly significant.* Jesus was telling Judas that he knew who it was directly, unmistakably, and for the first time (before this the warnings had all been general). Furthermore, "it was the custom for the host to show special honour or favour to one of his guests by dipping a choice morsel in the dish and handing this to him".[9] By choosing this method of identifying the betrayer Jesus was assuring him, even at this terrible time, of his love.

The Synoptic Gospels have a somewhat different account. St. Matthew (Matt. 26:20-25) in particular, tells us that in response to Jesus' statement that one will betray him, the disciples, ending with Judas, ask, "Is it I, Lord?" Jesus answers Judas "You have said so". Was this a public announcement? It is obvious from the events following (the fact that Judas assumed he could retain his anonymity and arranged to betray Jesus with a kiss) that it was not, i.e. that Our Lord's identification of Judas as the betrayer was not known by the other disciples.

To continue the analysis of John 13:21-30, in verse 27, we are told that Satan entered the heart of Judas after the morsel. Once again, how did the author know this? It could have been a sensible deduction based upon subsequent events. But if so, a scrupulous author(s) (and assuming the author(s) is scrupulous unless proven otherwise) would not have included such unnecessary conjecture. Even those who don't agree that the authorship was essentially the stamp of one person find it hard to explain why a redactor would add this kind of superfluous information.

To be sure Luke does use this phrase (Luke 22:3) but as an author he is far more inclined to use this kind of language as a literary device. Luke may have been contrasting Judas and Peter (Luke 22:31); Satan did not enter Peter, he did Judas. On the other hand, if the author were Judas, then he would have known and might have wanted to specify this as the moment when the decision became irrevocable in his own mind. And, knowing this, and wanting to justify, at least to some degree, his action, he placed part of the blame on Satan[10] (Judas being once again an involuntary agent). Following the giving of the morsel Jesus says to Judas, "What you are going to do, do quickly". This was overheard by the others and they assumed another meaning. Thus, again, it is obvious from the Fourth Gospel that the disciples hadn't heard or made the association between Judas and

---

[9] Temple, page 218.

[10] Bultmann, page 482. "Both of these have the effect of taking the act out of the sphere of human psychologically motivated action. It is not the man who is acting here, but Satan himself, the antagonist of God and the Revealer". *The Gospel of John: A Comentary.*

the betrayer. This is rather strange, since the identification and the "do quickly" came fairly close together. Even though the conversation may have lapsed or been lapsed or been interspersed with other conversations which are not given, it is still strange that the disciples didn't make the association. Was it because of all people they least expected the "Beloved Disciple" to be the betrayer?

There is great poignancy in the words, "So, after receiving the morsel, he immediately went out; and it was night."[11] This might have occurred to any sensitive observer, but is far more apt to have impressed the memory of the one to whom it happened. Judas's leaving was not at the time thought to have any unusual significance and so it was less likely that one not knowing that he was the betrayer would have made the observation even in retrospect. "He immediately went out and it was night" is obviously not a comment on the time of day, but a dramatic rendering which would be more apt to occur to the traitor than anyone else.

The fact that Judas left at this time would partially explain, if he were the author, the omission of the institution of the Last Supper. This is also explained on the basis that he might have left out those portions of the Synoptics which he felt adequately covered. But it would also be explained by his reluctance to relate something of which he wasn't an eyewitness. If we accept this latter explanation then we have to deal with the question raised by the material in 13:17-31. Bultmann[12], for different reasons, of course, believes these chapters belong to "Revelation-Discourses", one of the Sources of the Gospel. If this is so, then it is possible to explain the inclusion of 13:17-31 on the basis that the author was using materials for which he had a high regard and for this reason was willing to include even though he wasn't an eyewitness. Thus the account of the Last Supper was omitted, and the material in 13:17-31 included, for different, and not opposed reasons.

This whole incident (13:21-30 John) is recorded with a vivid detail that is typical of the author of the Fourth Gospel. That is, vis-à-vis the Synoptics, we often acquire in the Fourth Gospel *a greater sense of being there*, particularly in the reporting of conversational detail (e.g. Nicodemus, the Samaritan woman at the well, etc.). But what is interesting, further, is that the character of Judas, and

---

[11] Dodd, page 402 says "The sentence (13:30) is not only intensely dramatic, it also recalls the whole symbolism of light and darkness in the Book of Signs (cf ix. 4:) the agent of death who goes out into the night is the one who loves darkness rather than light because his deeds are evil (iii:19)". C. H. Dodd, *The Interpretation of the Fourth Gospel.*

[12] Bultmann, *The Gospel of John: A Commentary*, page 489. "A text from the 'revelation-discourses' forms the basis of the prayer, as it does the basis of the discourses to follow". In his revised order the "prayer" (17:2-26) comes before the "discourses" (13:31-16:33).

his role in the proceedings, becomes central in the Johannine narrative. In the Synoptics, although they vary considerably within themselves, the emphasis is on the betrayal, and the pathos centred on the other disciples ("Is it I, Lord?") and the matter of betrayal rather than the betrayer. It is interesting, also, to note that Mark's Gospel does not mention Judas by name saying, "For the Son of Man goes as it is written of him, but woe to that man by whom the Son of Man is betrayed! It would have been better for that man if he had not been born". (Mark 14:21). If this was indeed said by Jesus (and it is reported only in Mark) then Judas might well have wanted to forget it.

An important question remains. If this is all true then why did the author adopt the device of the Beloved Disciple?[13] This is gone into in greater detail elsewhere but is particularly important in this incident. The short answer is that he felt that he had to conceal his identity from the early church. If this is granted (and the identity of Judas and the Beloved Disciple assumed) then it can be seen that the description is very carefully and indeed cleverly written.

(D) *In the High Priestly Prayer Jesus refers to Judas* 17:12

"While I was with them, I kept them in thy name which thou hast given me; I have guarded them, and none of them is lost but the son of perdition that the scripture might be fulfilled." The only comment that needs to be made here is that if Judas were trying to justify what he had done, to himself or others, one justification could be that he was an involuntary agent of Scriptural prophecy. Did Jesus really pray that, or were the words put into his prayer by an author who wanted to justify his own actions?

(E) *Gethsemane* 18:2-11

When Jesus had spoken these words, he went forth with his disciples across the Kidron valley, where there was a garden, which he and his disciples entered. Now Judas, who betrayed him, also knew the place; for Jesus often met there with his disciples. So Judas, procuring a band of soldiers and some officers from the chief priests and the Pharisees, went there with lanterns and torches and weapons. Then Jesus, knowing all that was to befall him, came forward and said to them, "Whom do you seek?" They answered him, "Jesus of Nazareth". Jesus said to them, "I am he". Judas, who betrayed him, was standing with them. When he said to them "I am he", they drew back and fell to the ground, Again he asked them "Whom

---

[13] William Barclay in *The Master's Men* mentions the theory that Judas is the Beloved Disciple but says, "the identification of Judas and the Beloved Disciple is rendered impossible by the narrative of John 13:21-30 where the two characters are obviously different

do you seek?" And they said, "Jesus of Nazareth". Jesus answered, "I told you that I am he; so if you seek me, let these men go". This was to fulfil the word which he had spoken, "Of those whom thou gavest me I lost not one." Then Simon Peter, having a sword, drew it and struck the high priest's slave and cut off his right ear. The slave's name was Malchus. Jesus said to Peter, "Put your sword into its sheath; shall I not drink the cup which the Father has given me?"

It is worth noting that the author of the Fourth Gospel begins his account of what happened at the Garden of Gethsemane with the arrest of Jesus. There is no reference to Jesus' prayer as reported in the synoptics (Mark 14:32-42 and parallels). The author often omits events recorded in the Synoptic Gospels, perhaps as has been supposed he saw no need to put down again that which had already been adequately reported. That having been said, Judas would not have been there while Jesus was praying (being occupied in bringing those who made the arrest to the scene) and the prayer would have been a gap in his personal knowledge.

Considering the incident of the arrest as a whole, the record is confused. The Fourth Gospel does not mention the kiss. Matthew and Mark say that Judas kissed Jesus. Luke implies strongly that he did not. What was the source of the information about the kiss? It must have been one of the soldiers or arresting officers, or someone, at any rate, associated with the chief priests and Pharisees. It is highly unlikely that any of the evangelists heard this firsthand. But it was the kind of fact which would have been eagerly picked up and relayed after the event. Could we not suppose the following? Judas went to the Pharisees and high priests to take them to Gethsemane. He didn't want to be identified as the traitor, at least at the time, although he must have realized that he could only delay the discovery, not prevent it. So they agreed that he would kiss Jesus. This would be positive identification even in the dark; it was a customary greeting by a disciple to his Rabbi. Also, in the dark there would be the possibility of Judas taking[14] them to the Garden, leaving them, joining the disciples band unobtrusively and from that place kissing Jesus without necessarily being associated with the group came to arrest Jesus. That was what was planned. But what happened was that when the band arrived, Jesus ("knowing all that was to befall him", of course) stepped forward. There was no need to identify him. He identified himself. So the author of the Fourth Gospel (Judas) didn't bother to

---

[14] Brown, page 807. In support of this line of reasoning, Brown observes (Judas took), "Here the participle 'taking' implies little more than accompaniment as a guide". *The Gospel According to St. John* (2 vols, Raymond E. Brown.

record the method of identification since it hadn't been required or done. The synoptic sources (that is, Matthew and Mark), on the other hand, having heard that Judas was to betray him with a kiss, assumed that what was planned had, in fact, happened. The possibility of confusion in the darkness, and under the circumstances, would have been great. An alternative explanation is that Judas did kiss Jesus but that the author of the Fourth Gospel (Judas – beloved disciple) found this very distasteful to remember and contented himself with the synoptic recording of it.

There are two points to make in regard to this incident. The fact that there was a kiss, intended or actual, shows that Judas meant the betrayal to be anonymous. Otherwise, it would have been far easier just to point him out. Pointing him out could have been done verbally, or by gesture. But in either case, the gesture or the words would have if seen or overheard (and it would be difficult to ensure that this wouldn't have happened) drawn attention to the relationship between Judas and the arresting party. But with a kiss was different. It was an act of respect, of affection, and was well designed to disguise the betrayal. That is the best reason for the kiss. It was a well-thought-out manoeuvre. As has been said, he could not realistically have expected his anonymity to continue, although he might have deluded himself into thinking so (e.g. Nixon on Watergate). Further, there is no reason to assume he wasn't successful in concealing his identity for the time. Our mental image of the arrest is of Judas arriving at the head of the procession, in full torchlight, walking brazenly up to Jesus, handing him over with a kiss, in full view of soldiers and disciples, and standing by while Peter cut off the ear of Malchus. That mental image doesn't accord with all the facts, and it hardly could have happened that way. What we have is the record written in the light of later knowledge of Judas' betrayal, with, in the Synoptics' case, little knowledge, or interest, in Judas' location or movements. If they had known at the time that Judas was betraying Jesus, would not there have been some attempt, even on the part of these followers of Jesus, to prevent it or to do harm to Judas? A traitor often attracts more violent hatred than the person or cause he betrays for. At the time of the American Revolution, long after Britain and America were reconciled, the traitor Benedict Arnold was living in misery, despised by Americans and Englishmen alike. In 1950, most Englishmen would have had less trouble being civil to Stalin than to the turncoat spy Donald Maclean.

The disciples were ready enough to attack the arresting soldiers even though Jesus did not want or need that. Surely, if they had known at the time that Judas was the betrayer, they would have said something then which would have found its way into at least one of our Gospels. The Synoptic Gospels were written afterwards and in the knowledge that Judas betrayed, but that knowledge was acquired later.

The second point is in the identification in the Fourth Gospel by name of the slave (Malchus) whose ear was cut off by Peter. Why put this minor fact into the record? There were plenty of minor characters in the Gospel story whose names might have been well-known who could have been so designated. Furthermore, the name of the servant was not likely to have been known by the disciples or the early Christian community. It was a fact of little importance, unlikely to be remembered and less likely to be included unless it had some other significance. That other significance might be this. The name of the servant might well have been known by Judas. He had been to the Chief Priest to arrange for the betrayal. He might well have had personal contact with the servant. At a later stage we will go into the reasons why Judas wanted to conceal, and why he wanted to reveal, his authorship of the Fourth Gospel. Suffice it to say here that his was a cipher, a clue, for those who might want to know. So he included this fact that he, among the disciples, was more likely to know.

(F) *Summary*

Let us summarize this chapter on the incidents in which Judas appears in the Fourth Gospel. Firstly, in four of the incidents *the author of the Fourth Gospel knows something that only Judas would be apt to know.* In the first incident (6:70-71) the author knew that Jesus was talking about Judas when he foretold that one would betray him. Obvious to anyone? Not necessarily, but even if it were it would hardly have been necessary to record except that it would have been a very significant moment for Judas himself. In the second incident, the author knows that Judas didn't really care for the poor (12:6).

It could be that the author, if not Judas, simply wanted to heap calumny on calumny, or that he had later evidence that Judas was a thief. But if he had such evidence, why not state it in context, or can we believe that the author would slander (even Judas) just to further blacken his name.

On the other hand, there is only one place that such information could have incontrovertibly come from – Judas himself. In the third incident, the conversation during the preliminary stages of the Last Supper (the subject of so much confusion, discussion and ingenuity) becomes clear if we assume that Judas and the Beloved Disciple are one. Once again we have here a fact that only Judas could have known surely, "Satan entered into him" (13:27). In the fourth incident (the arrest) once more the whole becomes clearer if we assume Judas is the author, and there is the puzzling inclusion of the name of the slave whose ear was cut off. Who would have known this better than Judas?

71

Secondly *is the care that is taken to identify Judas*. He is described three times as the "son of Simon Iscariot" (6:71, 13:2, 13:26) and at critical points. At all other times, the phrase, "who betrayed him" or the equivalent is added parenthetically (12:4, 18:2, 18:5) except when in the sentence before he had been so designated (13:29, 18:3). In addition, care is taken not to confuse Judas Iscariot with the other Judas (14:22). *It is evident that the author was concerned to make certain that there was no mistake in identity.*

Thirdly, another important point is the prominent role that Satan plays in relation to Judas. Jesus used the terms Satan, Beelzebub, demon, devil, evil one, unclean spirits, son of perdition to describe the presence of evil.[15] Thus it was a man with "demons" who met Jesus in the country of the Gerasenes (Luke 8:26-39 and parallels). He spoke of the return of "evil spirits" to replace the "evil spirit" gone out of a man (Matt 12:43-45, Luke 11:24-26). Interestingly, however, there are only a few times when Jesus refers to a follower as being possessed in this way. One is after Peter's confession when Jesus then had to rebuke Peter saying, "Get behind me Satan". The other times he refers to possession of a follower by evil are in reference to Judas. When the betrayal was forecast after the feeding of the 5,000, Jesus refers to Judas as a "devil" (6:70); at the Last Supper we read "the devil had already put it into the heart of Judas" (13:2) and that "Satan entered him" after the morsel was given. In the High Priestly prayer Jesus refers to Judas as "the son of perdition". Even considering the fact that this was the common explanation for evil and evil acts used by Our Lord, the frequency and vehemence of such references is worthy of comment. One explanation is the natural desire by the author to condemn the traitor. The question that needs to be asked then is why he went into such detail to identify not only the fact that Satan entered Judas, but the time this happened as well as the earlier time it was put into his heart. Judas would be best situated to know this, but, further, he might have had a particular interest in describing himself as an involuntary agent of Satan, performing a role ordained from the beginning. This would have been one explanation for what he did, one way to partially escape personal responsibility.

Fourthly, is the prominent role that Judas plays in the Johannine account of two major events in Jesus' ministry, the Upper Room and Gethsemane.

---

[15] In considering this we should not be put off by the terms "Satan" or "devil" or "son of perdition". The problem of evil is real. Today we might use different terminology, e.g. the nomenclature of psychiatry, talk in terms of motivation, intention, time of decision, etc. Jesus used the language of his time and it can be seen as a convenient shorthand for our understanding. To say that Satan entered Judas at a certain time may be to say, in effect, that it was at that time that Judas made a decision to do something that was evil.

Chapter IV

New Testament References to Judas

Next, we examine the references to Judas in the rest of the New Testament. Are there differences between the Fourth Gospel and the Synoptics in their presentation of Judas? If so, what are these and what is their significance?

(A) Following is a list of the places where Judas is referred to – by name, as "betrayer", or as "traitor":

Incident or Setting	Mt.	Mk.	Lk.	John	Acts
(1) Call of the twelve	10:1-4	3:13-19	6:12-16		1:13 (listing of 11)
(2) Betrayal Forecast				6:70,71	
(3) Anointing by Mary				12:1-8	
(4) Judas goes to Chief Priests	26:14-16	14:10-11	22:3-6		
(5) "Is it I, Lord"	26:20-25	14:17-21	22:21-23		
Last supper				13 (13:23-25)	
(6) Gethsemane	26:47-56	14:43-52	22:47-53	18:2-11	
(7) (In the court of the high priest)				18:15-16 "another disciple"	
(8) Judas' replacement as apostle & death	27:3-10				1:15-20
(9) Crucifixion				(19:25-27)	
(10) (Empty tomb)				(20:1-10)	
(11) Resurrection Appearance at Sea of Tiberias)				(21)	

( ) indicate incidents and passages where Beloved Disciple appears in the Fourth Gospel.

(B) Consideration of Incidents

(1) *Call of the twelve.* Judas is given as one of the twelve in each listing in the Synoptics of the Twelve; he is identified as he "who betrayed him" (Matthew and Mark) or the "traitor" (Luke). His name is the last to appear in each list. He is not named in the list of eleven in Acts 1:13.

(2) *Judas Goes to the Chief Priests.* All three Synoptics tell of how Judas went to the chief priests, how he was promised money, and how he sought the opportunity to betray Jesus. Luke adds the interesting detail (Luke 22:3) that it was at this time that "Satan entered his heart". Luke also tells us that they sought an opportunity to betray him in the absence of the multitude. This is relevant since it is a necessity for betrayal. Mark has an interesting textural idiosyncrasy. In Mark 14:10 there is an extra article. Barclay[1] comments. It could mean "the (chief) one of the twelve" and indicate that Judas held the top position among the twelve. If so, it would have been inexplicable to later generations (editors and translators) and it is easy to see why it might have been expunged. It is possible that Judas was the natural leader of the apostolic band (treasurers often are!) but later generations would have preferred to forget this.

It could mean other things. The other interesting point about the Synoptic accounts of Judas going to the chief priests is that it follows (in Mark and Matthew) the anointing at Bethany. The Fourth Gospel doesn't tell of Judas going to the chief priests to arrange for the betrayal, but he appears prominently as Judas in the account of the anointing. Would we be correct in assuming that there was some connection between this incident and Judas' going to the chief priests?[2] Matthew and Mark don't report Judas' objection to the expense of the ointment, but do have the apostles objecting for the same reason. They leave Judas out altogether.

(3) *The Last Supper.* In considering the Last Supper, the following charts the main events recorded by the Evangelists. The evidence as to the order of the events is very slender. The following is a rough approximation:

---

[1] Barclay, page 74, see also Gore p. 106 (NT section) who says it can mean Judas who was one of the twelve (in contrast with Judas of James).

[2] Did the anointing trigger Judas' action in contacting the chief priests? If so, the clue as to why might lie in the Fourth Gospel account of the anointing. A possible reason is found in the "Reconstruction".

The Last Supper – Main Events[3]

Event	Mt.	Mk.	Lk.	John
Betrayal foretold	26:20-22	14:18-31	(22:21-23)	13:1-3 (18)
Footwashing				13:3-20
Disciples ask "Is it I, Lord?"	26:20-25	14:17-21	22:(22-23)	13:21-30
Judas leaves[3]				13:31
Institution	26:26-29	14:22-25	22:14-20	
		(9:34ff)		
Greatness in the Kingdom	(20:25-28)	(10:42-45)	22:24-30	
	(18:1)			
Peter's denial prophesied			22:31-34	13:36-38
Two swords			22:35-38	
(Peter's denial prophesied on				
Road to Gethsemane)	(26:30-35)	(14:26-31)		

There are three conclusions to be drawn from this.

First, the fact that the instution of the Last Supper is left out of John would lead us to think that the author, or redactor, of the Fourth Gospel edited his writing in the light of the Synoptic tradition. It is hard to see him leaving out the Last Supper entirely unless he knew that it was part of the Synoptic tradition. The inclusion of the footwashing, in fair detail, was then seen as especially desirable because it was not in the Synoptics, and as it shed additional light on Peter's character (a concern of the author).

Second, the Fourth Gospel leaves out entirely the fact recorded in the Synoptics that the disciples asked, "Is it I, Lord?" If Judas were the author this would be explained by his consternation at that point (at Jesus' prediction that one of them would betray him). We can understand that he might not have heard the disciples questioning themselves), or thought it irrelevant material since they had obviously not betrayed him, and he and Jesus knew who the betrayer was.

Third, is there any significance in the fact that Matthew (alone of the Synoptics) records Judas also as asking, but his words are, "Is it I, *Rabbi?*" The other disciples replied, "Is it I, Lord?" Judas also called Jesus, "Rabbi" when he spoke to him in Gethsemane (according to the Synoptics).

---

[3] Westcott, page 188, thinks Judas may have left between the giving of the bread and the cup. The Lukan order differs substantially from that in Mark. Luke 22:21-23 represents a difficulty in the order and this is indicated by giving several locations in parentheses. The Marcan and Matthean accounts of "Greatness in the Kingdom" occur earlier, but references are given, also in parentheses.

See also Brown, pages 581-604; Dodd, *Interpretation of the Fourth Gospel*, 390-421.

(4) *Gethsemane*. The next incident in which the Synoptics mention Judas is at Gethsemane. It is not essential to this study to maintain that the disciples did not realize at the time that Judas led the band to Jesus, but it makes more reasonable the assumption that Judas (pseudonym, Beloved Disciple) was there at the Cross, the Empty Tomb and the Sea of Tiberias. Let us test this against what the Gospels say. Luke (22.47) is the only Gospel which actually says that Judas was leading them. This could be explained in several different ways. First, that Judas was out in front and seen as such. Second that Luke had a separate tradition, based upon the recollection of an apostle or a member of the arresting force who saw it this way. Even so, this might not have become general information until days or weeks after the event. Third that Luke simply drew a (wrong) conclusion from the Marcan narrative.

The two other Gospels say that Judas came with the arresting force In either case (Luke or Matthew-Mark) it is reasonable to assume that this information was acquired after the event and then put into the record to show that it was, in fact, Judas who betrayed Jesus. Once again, the fact that Judas had arranged a code (the kiss, a sign between them, a concerted signal)[4] to identify Jesus indicates that he intended to retain his anonymity. If so, we can hardly picture him marching up at the head of the procession. In the dark, lighted only by torches, it would have been relatively easy to remain anonymous, and to mingle with either group.

It is significant that in Mark, Judas says (14:44) "seize (take, or arrest) him and lead him away *safely?* "Why would Judas be concerned at that point with Jesus' *safety*". It surely wasn't only his immediate safety he was concerned with. Why spare a man who was about to die a little indignity on the way? The arresting force was irregular, but surely the chief priests couldn't have openly condoned or risked harm coming to Jesus at this point. They must have at least the pretence of a hearing.

The scenario that I have sketched is that he betrayed Jesus for any, or a combination of, several possible reasons, e.g. because he agreed partly with the arguments of the Pharisees and the high priests, because he thought the situation was getting out of hand and there might be an insurrection, for Jesus' own safety, because Jesus had overstepped the mark in his claims, and because of his lack of trust in Jesus' judgment.

If this is so, he didn't believe he hated the Lord, and thought he didn't want him to come to real harm. The use of the word "safely" here would indicate that to be the case. Matthew and Luke may have left out "safely" because they would

---

[4] *The Gospel According to St. Mark*, Rev. Ezra P. Gould.

see little point in Judas' concern in the light of the crucifixion. But there is no need to assume that Judas betrayed Jesus knowing he would be crucified. He may well have done the deed thinking Jesus' fate would be any of several other possibilities (an informal reprimand, protective custody, excommunication).[5]

In retrospect, none of this seems probable but Judas didn't have the advantage of hindsight and was a victim of self-deception, in any case. The crucifixion was inevitable. At the time, for any of the apostles, it was only a nightmarish possibility.

W. H. Vanstone in *The Stature of Waiting* has some interesting thoughts on the Greek verb παρ-αδίδωμι which has been translated as meaning Judas betrayed Jesus. Citing the various places where it is used not only in reference to Judas' act but also of Jesus death on the Cross where Jesus "bowed his head and *handed over* His spirit," he says, "Whatever the reason for the familiar mistranslation of παρ-αδίδωμι as 'betray', it remains a mistranslation. The verb is ambivalent, neutral, colourless; and we shall continue to translate it as 'to hand over'".[6]

Thus, it is the premise in this section on the "betrayal" at Gethsemane that what became clearer later on was not clear at all at the time. There is good reason to believe that the act of betrayal (the kiss) was not seen as that at the time. The Markan phrase "lead him away safely" as well as the better translation of παρ-αδίδωμι as "to hand over" give us a clue that Judas' motives may have been more complex and ambivalent than portrayed in the Gospels which reflected the Church's desire to simplify and make Judas the scapegoat.

(5) *Judas' Death.* We note the Fourth Gospel has no account of Judas' death; notable, since the author tells us so much about him and he had such an important role in the Upper Room and at the arrest.

Judas' death is reported in two places, Matthew 27:3-10 and Acts 1:15-20. About the death itself, Kirsopp Lake, after examining the two accounts, and considering the additional account in Papias, and also parallels in Old Testament and ancient literature, concludes:

"Early narratives as to the death of men distinguished either for good or bad qualities are always liable to be coloured by the literary tradition as to similar persons. This fact certainly has its bearing on the story of the death of Judas. From the complete contradiction between the three narratives,

---

[5] See Hastings *Bible Dictionary* page 278 for various types of punishment current in Jesus' day, also p. 86 under "Ban".
[6] W. H. Vanstone, *Stature of Waiting*, page 7.

which do not fully agree on any point and which differ sharply on most, it is clear that we have not much real recollection of fact".[7]

That would seem to be conclusive about the death itself. It would seem a classic case of the wish being handmaid to the deed and there is no need to even assume that Judas died. As Mark Twain commented, "the reports of my death have been greatly exaggerated".

Of more interest than the reputed death of Judas is the account in Acts 1:15-20 of what Peter says in regard to Judas.

(1) Judas in betraying Jesus was an agent of Scriptural prophecy.

(2) He must be replaced so that the apostolic number might be restored so that he may with the others be a witness to the resurrection (1:21-22).

Both conclusions are buttressed by quotations from the Psalms (1:16). We can conclude from (1) above that the early Church was searching for a reason as to why a man chosen as a disciple by Jesus should then betray him. We can (perhaps) see in (2) above a desire to replace and therefore forget about Judas and get on with the work of the Church.

(6) *Summary.* There are few general conclusions that can be drawn from the material about Judas in the New Testament, apart from the Fourth Gospel. It is true that there is little about him. The Synoptics have very little additional information. They mention Judas only where it is absolutely necessary to the narrative. This is not surprising since they don't give us much information about most of the disciples. Most of such information comes from the Fourth Gospel.

It may well be significant that, as Vanstone points out, it is better rendered "to hand over" than "to betray". If so, and combined with the otherwise strange Markan phrase "lead him away safely", it can be argued that Judas' motives were complex and ambiguous and the early Church simplified this,[8] in the natural human tendency to present the situation in black and white, good and evil, and

---

[7] *The Beginnings of Christianity Part I. The Acts of the Apostles* by Foakes Jackson and Kirsopp Lake Vol. 5 Additional Note IV.

[8] Vanstone's comment on Judas' betrayal (p.4) is "And yet, as we have seen, the deed cannot have been of major importance in a strictly historical sense: it cannot in itself have determined or changed the course of events. It began to seem to me, therefore, that the Gospel writers might be representing the deed of Judas as important in something other than a strictly historical sense: as important in a symbolic or theological sense: as important not in accounting for what happened in the last hours of Jesus' life but in expressing the meaning of what happened".

to shift the responsibility away from others. Thus some of the Germans after WW2 at all levels of society were content to put the blame solely on Adolf Hitler.

More significant is the fact that there is so little about Judas other than in the Gospels. He is mentioned by name only once (Acts 1:16). Reference to him at this point could hardly be avoided since they were choosing his successor. He is referred to as the "betrayer" only once, in I Corinthians 11:23. If there is any argument from silence, it is that the early Christian community (as evolving in the tradition behind the Synoptics as well as the situation seen in the Epistles) wanted to forget about Judas, and largely did so. There is little legendary material about him. He became a non-person. This makes sense. Being Christians, they couldn't condone hatred. He was an enigma, but not a very important one compared to the news they had to spread. They ignored and forgot him, made him dead.

The crux of this study, the most intriguing question in the whole of Biblical studies, is the enigma of the Beloved Disciple. Who was he? But underlying this "Who" question, and preliminary to the "who" question, is the "Why" question. It is the premise of this study that only in answering the question of *Why* the Beloved Disciple device is used can we answer intelligibly the question of *"Who"* he was. Thus a detective looks for motivation as the first clue as to who the criminal might be.

The fundamental premise of the investigation of the *Why* and the *Who* question is that the author of the Fourth Gospel is "not the expression of a community with many voices, but above all the voice of a towering theologian, the founder and head of the Johannine school".[9]

---

[9] Martin Hengel. *The Johannine Question*, page IX.

Chapter V

Internal Evidence of Authorship

What does the author of the Fourth Gospel say about himself? Is this credible, or what reliance can we place on it? What is its significance?

The author of the Fourth Gospel feels it necessary to refer to himself in a way unique in the Gospels. These occur as follows:

(1) John 20:30-31

Now Jesus did many other signs in the presence of the disciples, which are not written in this book, but these are written so that you may believe that Jesus is the Christ, the son of God, and that believing you may have life in his name.

(2) John 21:24-25

This is the disciple who is bearing witness to these things, and who has written these things and we know that his testimony is true.

In addition, there are two other, less important, references:

(1) The "we" in John 1:14

And the word became flesh and dwelt among us, full of grace and truth, we have beheld his glory, as of the only Son from the Father.

(2) John 19:32-35

So the soldiers came and broke the legs of the first, and of the other who had been crucified with him; but when they came to Jesus and saw that he was already dead, they did not break his legs. But one of the soldiers pierced his side with a spear, and at once there came out blood and water. He who saw it has borne witness – his testimony is true, and he knows that he tells the truth – that you also may believe.

The author refers to authorship in two passages. The first of these is at the end of Chapter 20, verses 30 and 31:

"Now Jesus did many other signs in the presence of the disciples, which are not written in this book; but these are written that you may believe that Jesus is the Christ, the Son of God and that believing you may have life in his name".

If the Gospel were to end with this chapter we would regard this as a fitting conclusion. In these two verses we are told that all has not been said, and we are told the purpose in writing. What exactly he meant by "signs" has been subject for discussion. "Signs" is an important word in the Johannine vocabulary, and in the analysis of the Gospel. The purpose of the Gospel is stated in verse 31 and it follows the thought of the prior incident, the demonstration to Thomas of the resurrection. In this incident, Thomas is seen as able to make certain of the reality of the resurrection by seeing Jesus' body, and the wounds on it, and by placing his hand in Jesus' side. Then the Lord (20:29) says this, "Have you believed because you have seen me? Blessed are those who have not seen and yet believe". The author then picks up this thought by explaining that his Gospel is written so that the reader may believe. He wants us, however, to believe in a certain theology, that Jesus is the Christ, the Son of God. He was the Jewish Messiah, but he was more than that, "the Word became flesh", the Son of God. Yet, even belief in Jesus as Messiah and Son of God is not enough. Belief leads to life, also an important word in the Johannine vocabulary.

Thus the Gospel might end. But we have another chapter. The great majority of commentators believe that this additional chapter is an appendix. The debate is about who added it, and why. Again, for our purpose it isn't necessary to do more than note the existence of the problem the appendix poses.

At the end of Chapter 21 we also find another concluding statement:

"This is the disciple who is bearing witness to these things, and who has written these things; and we know that his testimony is true. But there are also many other things which Jesus did; were every one of them to be written, I suppose that the world itself could not contain the books that would be written".

Once again, who wrote it and why? What is its relationship to the similar, but less complete, statement at the end of Chapter 20? In looking at these verses we note, that as in the similar summary statement at the end of Chapter 20, there is a definite connection with what precedes. This need not have been so. The summary could have appeared without any such connection, as a summary of the author's purpose in the writing of the whole of the Gospel. Here the connection is even more important to the statement. For the author (redactor) of this summary statement (verses 24, 25) wants to tie the authorship to the "Beloved Disciple" who, in this resurrection incident, plays such a prominent part. This statement, in verse 24, says it is the idea that he "is bearing witness". This is, in most cases, as eyewitness, in others his personal assurance that the witness of others is accurate, that he has, in other words, a spiritual and primary responsibility for the whole. Furthermore, he has not only "borne witness" he has "written these things". The argument as to whether he has actually written them in his own hand is not important to our purpose. The fact is that whether this is interpreted literally or not, the redactor says that the author is responsible for the writing.

"We know that his testimony is true". Who are the "we"? It would seem on the face of it to involve more than one person who has been associated with the author and knew him well enough to be able to vouch for his work. This almost necessarily would mean that they had helped in that work, or knew it well. We cannot expect that they would have given carte blanche to something so important if they had not known it well and at least had the opportunity to make editorial comments. The group has been identified with the Johannine disciples (sometimes called the "Ephesian elders".[1]

The next verse (25) does not necessarily follow the preceding verse, but it certainly is an appropriate thought at this point and there is no need to assume that it is displaced. It would seem to be a rewriting of the statement in 20:30-31 to emphasize again that the author makes no claim to include everything (that would be impossible), particularly in the way the Fourth Gospel is written, giving us not only the bare bones of what happened, with the fleshing these out with insight into the meaning, both by explicit statements and by use of dialogue and by the skill of a dramatist (who, however, does not invent the drama but exposes it by his skill). This verse (25) does also give evidence that the redactor is concerned that the Gospel not be faulted on any account, not even by the charge that things (important matters) have been left out. The author has crafted his Gospel to do what he believes he has been inspired by the Spirit to do, give a balanced and measured account of the Good News.

Some commentators believe that the summary statement (21:25) applies only to the last chapter. This is held particularly by those who believe Chapter 21 as a whole is by another hand. However, would a conscientious author, or redactor, put such a conclusions on the end of the Gospel unless he meant it to apply to the whole? This is a valid question even if there was some period of time between the original compilation and the work of the redactor.

---

[1] Brown, page 1124.

The "we" in 1:14 and the "He" in 19:32-35.

There are two other places where the author refers in some way to witnesses:
"And the Word became flesh and dwelt among us, full of grace and truth; we have beheld his glory, glory as of the only Son from the Father". (1:14).
"So the soldiers came and broke the legs of the first, and of the other who had been crucified with him; but when they came to Jesus and saw that he was already dead, they did not break his legs. But one of the soldiers pierced his side with a spear, and at once there came out blood and water. *He* who saw it has borne witness – his testimony is true, and *he* knows that he tells the truth – that you also may believe" (19:32-35).

The first of these is relevant (to our purpose) in that it shows the author's desire to make even the most theological of statements in the Gospels (the Prologue) a matter, also, of personal witness. It is interesting to compare this with the sentiment expressed in 1 John 1:1-3. There is no way of determining who the "we" is, although it would seem to be those among whom Jesus exercised his earthly ministry, rather than a limited group of Johannine disciples.

The second of the statements above interrupts the narrative of the Gospel at an important point to make a claim for eyewitness. Was it the author who saw this and is using the third person to express it? Again we have no way of knowing for certain. But it would seem a clue may be in the question, "Why this statement at this point?" One answer is the miraculous nature of the spear bringing forth blood and water. Did the author expect that the reader would question the authenticity of this? I would think that is the only reasonable explanation for such an editorial comment at this point. The person ("He who saw it and has borne witness") might be the author. More likely, since that would be true for much of the Gospel, including other miraculous sections, it was some other witness from whom the author obtained an account of this occurrence which he (the author) had not personally seen happen.

Summary

In the above references to authorship or eyewitness accounts three facts emerge clearly. (1) The author was concerned to ensure that the Gospel received authentication from the witness of those who were actually there. (2) The author wants to make this specific by making it clear that the Beloved Disciple is responsible for "writing" the Gospel. (3) He was concerned, always, that the Gospel should be seen not only as a narration of facts (a biography of Jesus) but that this truth be believed and that not in a sterile, purely intellectual way but that it become an occasion for life.

Keeping this in mind, the premise here is as follows: Judas–Beloved Disciple-author wrote the Gospel, chapters 1-20, perhaps in conjunction with others but mainly from his own experiences reflected upon during his time in isolation. He seems to have intended to conclude his Gospel with the brief summary statement in 20:30-31. But at the same time he had prepared Chapter 21. However, he did not feel able to include Chapter 21 at this time. Why? Because it contained a clue to the connection between Judas and Beloved Disciple. This was because of the nature of the resurrection appearance on the Sea of Tiberias. One of the disciples present must still be alive, or the story may have been told so that it would be possible to make the identification of Judas with the disciple named here as the one whom Jesus loved. We remember that the number of disciples at the Sea of Tiberias had been reduced, from twelve to seven. Thus it was much more likely that by process of elimination the identity of Judas and Beloved Disciple could be made. Perhaps some disinformation has been spread and this is why Papias (expanding on his source which must have been the Fourth Gospel) hazarded a guess as to who the two unnamed were.

So Judas had to wait to publish this last incident. This disciple could not have been Peter, because Peter could have made this identification in any case (because of the Empty Tomb, and the Chief Priest's court). On the other hand, the resurrection appearance was important. It was important for its own intrinsic worth, because it was such a vivid and detailed an account of one of Jesus' appearances after his resurrection, it was important for the Church's understanding of the apostle Peter and his role in the Church, and it was important for the Church's understanding of the Beloved Disciple.

So Judas–Beloved Disciple-author held this (our last chapter) up. The bulk of this Gospel hadn't been released, but he wanted it all in order in case he died. He left the additional chapter as an additional will and testament, along with instructions to John or (more likely) his other collaborators to publish the last chapter when he ascertained that it was safe. We cannot tell what happened then. Did Judas–Beloved Disciple-author die before the Gospel was released? If so, his spiritual heirs released it as a whole when they felt it was safe, and also wrote the summary statement (21:24-25). If Judas–Beloved Disciple-author lived to this point he did this himself (ascertained that it was safe to issue the last chapter and added the summary statement (21:24-25) and released the whole of the Gospel). They, the author and his associates, including John the Apostle and/or John the Elder, or John the Apostle who was John the Elder, were concerned to show that the Gospel as a whole was not only the product of individual effort but was supported by a wider group (the "we" of 21:24).

Chapter VI

External Evidence of Authorship

In this chapter consideration will be given to the evidence for John's authorship of the Fourth Gospel other than what is given in the Gospel itself. This is what is referred to as "external evidence". The main sources in the early Church are not numerous and are fairly brief. The references are printed below so that the reader will have some of the basic texts. It is important and useful to see the kind of evidence upon which the arguments are based. It should be noted from the start that scholars have debated the reliability and relative importance of these texts almost from the time they were written. Rarely in the history of Biblical criticism have so many said so much about so little. All is not as simple as it might seem!

I The Documents

Eusebius was Bishop of Caesarea c.A.D. 260-339. He is often called the "Father of Ecclesiastical History". In his work, *The History of the Church* he gives some of the first references to the authorship of the Fourth Gospel, as follows:

A **Papias,** c.60-130, Bishop of Hierapolis in Asia Minor. Only fragments of his work survive, quoted by Irenaeus and Eusebius. Here follows Eusebius (HE 3. 39):

"Papias has left us five volumns entitled, *The Sayings of the Lord Explained.* These are mentioned by Irenaeus as the only works from his pen:

'To these things Papias, who had listened to John and was later a companion of Polycarp, and who had lived at a very early date, bears written testimony in the fourth of his books; he composed five'.

This is what Irenaeus says; but Papias himself in the preface to his work makes it clear that he was never a hearer or eyewitness of the holy apostles, and tells us that he learnt the essentials of the Faith from their former pupils:

'I shall not hesitate to furnish you, along with the interpretations, with all that in days gone by I carefully learnt from the presbyters and have carefully recalled, for I can guarantee its truth. Unlike most people, I felt at home not with those who had a great deal to say, but with those who taught the truth; not with those who appeal to commandments from other sources but with those who appeal to the commandments given by the Lord to faith and coming to us from truth itself. And whenever anyone came who had been a follower of the presbyters, I inquired into the words of the presbyters, what Andrew or Peter had said, or Philip or Thomas or James or John or Matthew, or any other disciple of the Lord, and what Aristion and the presbyter John, disciples of the Lord, were still saying. For I did not imagine that things out of books would help me as much as the utterances of a living and abiding voice'".

B **Irenaeus**, Bishop of Lugdunum in Gaul (*c*.A.D. 130-200; he became Bishop *c*.A.D. 178), his chief work was *Adversus omnes Haereses*. He is here quoted in this passage by Eusebius (HE 3, 23):

"A story about John the apostle

In Asia, moreover, there still remained alive the one whom Jesus loved, apostle and evangelist alike, John, who had directed the churches there since his return from exile on the island following Domitian's death. That he survived so long is proved by the evidence of two witnesses who could hardly be doubted, ambassadors as they were of the orthodoxy of the Church – Irenaeus and Clement of Alexandria. In Book II of his *Against Heresies*, Irenaeus writes:

'All the clergy (elders) who in Asia came in contact with John, the Lord's disciple, testify that John taught the truth to them; for he remained with them til Trajan's time'. (Irenaeus *Against Heresies* II 33 2)

In Book III of the same work he says the same thing: 'The Church of Ephesus was founded by Paul, and John remained there til Trajan's time; so she is a true witness of what the apostle taught'." (Irenaeus *Against Heresies* III 3 4).

Clement, in addition to indicating the date, adds a story that should be familiar to all who like to hear what is noble and helpful. It will be found in the short work entitled "The Rich Man Who Finds Salvation". Turn up the passage, and read what he writes:

"Listen to a tale that not just a tale but a true account of John the apostle, handed down and remembered. When the tyrant was dead, and John had moved from the island of Patmos to Ephesus, he used to go when asked to the neighbouring districts of the Gentile peoples, sometimes to appoint bishops, sometimes to organize whole churches, sometime to ordain one person of those pointed out by the Holy Spirit". (Here follows a long tale of a young man whom John entrusted to the care of a bishop. The young man became a brigand and was later brought to repentance by John.)

Eusebius also quotes Irenaeus in the following passage (HE 5. 8, quoting Irenaeus *Adv. Haer.* iii, i, 1):

"Irenaeus' comments on Holy Scripture

At the beginning of the work I promised, when convenient, to quote passages in which the early presbyters and historians of the Church have transmitted in writing the traditions that had come down to them regarding the canonical scriptures. One of these was Irenaeus, so without more ado I will quote his remarks, beginning with those which concern the Holy Gospels.

'Matthew published a written gospel for the Hebrews in their own tongue, while Peter and Paul were preaching the gospel in Rome and founding the church there. After their passing, Mark also, the disciple and interpreter of Peter, transmitted to us in writing the things preached by Peter. Luke, the follower of Paul, set down in a book the gospel preached by him. Lastly John, the disciple of the Lord, **who had leant back on His breast**, once more set forth (exedwke, "published" or "gave out", but not "transmitted in writing" or "set down in a book", see above!) the gospel, while residing at Ephesus in Asia.'"

C **Polycarp** *c.*69-*c.*155, Bishop of Smyrna, burned to death when he had "served Christ for 86 years", may have been a child in A.D. 70-80 and could have heard eyewitnesses in addition to John of Ephesus.[1]

The next question to be asked is raised by the fact that Irenaeus, born about A.D. 130, did not know the people or events of which he was writing. What were his sources? Irenaeus tells us that Polycarp is one in this passage by Eusebius (He 4. 14):

"The story of Polycarp, the pupil of the apostles. At this period, while Anicetus was head of the Roman church, Polycarp, who was still living, came to Rome and discussed with Anicetus some difficulty about the date of Easter. This we gather from Irenaeus, who tells us another story about Polycarp which must be included in the account of him that I am giving. Here it is:

From Book III of *Against Heresies*, by Irenaeus

'Polycarp was not only instructed by apostles and conversant with many who had seen the Lord, but was appointed by apostles to serve in Asia as Bishop of Smyrna. I myself saw him in my early years, for he lived a long time and was very old indeed when he laid down his life by a glorious and

---

[1] Hengel, *The Johannine Question*, page 15.

most splendid martyrdom. At all times he taught the things which he had learnt from the apostles, which the Church transmits, which alone are true. These factors are attested by all the churches of Asia and by the successors of Polycarp to this day – and he was a much more trustworthy and dependable witness to the truth than Valentinus and Marcion and all other wrong-headed persons. In the time of Anicetus he stayed for a while in Rome, where he won over many from the camp of these heretics to the Church of God, proclaiming that the one and only truth he had received from the apostles was the trust transmitted by the Church. And there are people who heard him descibe how John, the Lord's disciple, when at Ephesus went to take a bath, but seeing Cerinthus inside rushed out of the building without taking a bath, crying: "let us get out of here, for fear the place falls in, now that Cerinthus, the enemy of truth, is inside!' Polycarp himself on one occasion came face to face with Marcion, and when Marcion said "Don't you recognize me?" he replied "I do indeed: I recognize the firstborn of Satan!" So careful were the apostles and their disciples to avoid even exchanging words with any falsifier of the truth, in obedience to the Pauline injunction: "If a man remains heretical after more than one warning, have no more to do with him, recognizing that a person of that type is a perverted sinner, self-condemned".

'There is also a most forceful epistle written by Polycarp to the Philippians, from which both the character of his faith and his preaching of the truth can be learnt by all who wish to do so and care about their own salvation.'

Such is Irenaeus' account. Polycarp in his letter to the Philippians, referred to above and still extant, has supported his views with several quotations from the First Epistle of Peter (HE 4. 14).

Eusebius also quotes Irenaeus' letter to Florinus as to Irenaeus relationship with Polycarp (HE 5. 20).

"When I was still a boy I saw you in Lower Asia in Polycarp's company, when you were cutting a fine figure at the imperial court and wanted to be in favour with him. I have a clearer recollection of events at that time than of recent happenings – what we learn in childhood develops along with the mind and becomes a part of it – so that I can describe the place where blessed Polycarp sat and talked, his goings out and comings in, the character of his life, his personal appearance, his addresses to crowded congregations. I remember how he spoke of his intercourse with John and with the others who had seen the Lord; how he repeated their words from memory; and how the things that he had heard them say about the Lord,

His miracles and His teaching, things that he had heard direct from the eye-witnesses of the Word of Life, were proclaimed by Polycarp in complete harmony with Scripture. To these things I listened eagerly at that time, by the mercy of God shown to me, not committing them to writing but learning them by heart. By God's grace, I constantly and conscientiously ruminate on them . . ."

D **Polycrates**, Bishop of Ephesus A.D. 189-98; little is known of him except that he opposed Pope Victor on when Easter should be celebrated. He is here quoted in another passage by Eusebius (HE 3. 31):

"The date of John's death has also been roughly fixed: the place where his mortal remains lie can be gathered from a letter of Polycrates, Bishop of Ephesus, to Victor, Bishop of Rome. In it he refers not only to John but to Philip the apostle and Philip's daughters as well:

'In Asia great luminaries sleep who shall rise again on the last day, the day of the Lord's Advent, when He is coming with glory from heaven and shall search out all His saints – such as Philip, one of the twelve apostles, who sleeps in Hierapolis with two of his daughters, who remained unmarried to the end of their days, while his other daughter lived in the Holy Spirit and rests in Ephesus. Again there is John, who leant back on the Lord's breast, and who became a priest wearing the mitre, a martyr and a teacher; he too sleeps in Ephesus'."

E **The Muratorian Canon** The oldest extant list of New Testament writings, generally considered to be dated 180-200:

"The fourth gospel is by John, one of the disciples. When his fellow-disciples and his bishops exhorted him he said, Today fast with me for three days, and let us recount to each other whatever may be revealed to each of us. That same night it was revealed to Andrew, one of the apostles, that John should write down all things under his name, as they all called them to mind (recogniscentibus cuntis, for recognoscentibus cunctis; perhaps 'revised' or 'certified'). So although various points are taught in the several books of the gospels, yet it makes no difference to the faith of believers, since all things in all of them are declared by one supreme Spirit, concerning (our Lord's) nativity, his passion, his resurrection, his converse with his disciples, and his twofold advent, the first in despised lowliness, which has taken place, and the second glorious with kingly power, which is yet to come. What wonder then if John so boldly sets forth each point, saying of himself in his epistles (in epistulis, for in epistolis; perhaps 'in his epistle'), What we have seen with our eyes and heard with our ears, and our hands have handled, these things we have written (scripsmus)? For so he avows himself to be not only an eye-witness and hearer (reading se et auditorem) but also a writer of all the wonderful works of the Lord in order".[2]

F **Jerome** c.342-420, first translated the Bible into Latin (Vulgate). The following reference to John the apostle is in Jerome's *Commentary on the Epistle to the Galatians* Westcott translation as given by Tasker):[3]
"When he tarried at Ephesus to extreme old age, and could only with difficulty be carried to the church in the arms of his disciples, and was unable to give utterance to many words, he used to say no more at their several meetings than this, 'Little children, love one another'. At length the disciples and fathers who were there, wearied with hearing always the same words, said, 'Master, why dost thou always say this?' 'It is the Lord's command', was his worthy reply, 'and if this alone be done, it is enough.'"

G **Anti-Marcionite Prologue to the Fourth Gospel.** This work, which must be used with caution, is thought to be a translation of a Greek original c.A.D. 150-200:
"The Gospel of John was **revealed** to the churches by John while he was still in the body, as Papias of Hierapolis, John's dear disciple, recorded in his five exegetical books. He wrote down the Gospel correctly at John's dictation. But the heretic Marcion, after he had been reproved by him for his contrary opinions, was rejected by John. He had brought him writings or letters from the brethren who were in Pontus".[4]

H **Other Evidence** Barratt[5] in his comprehensive summary of the external evidence also lists the evidence for the divergent tradition of John's early death. This is in conflict with the writings shown above which indicate that John lived to an old age in Ephesus. First there is Mark 10.38-9:
But Jesus said to them (the sons of Zebedee), "You do not know what you are asking, Are you able to drink the cup that I drink, or to be baptized with the cup with which I am baptized?" And they said to him, "We are able". And Jesus said to them, "The cup I drink you will drink, and with

[2] Barrett, page 114-5.
[3] Tasker, page 10.
[4] Sanders, page 36.
[5] Barrett, page 103.

the baptism with which I am baptized you will be baptized;"

This could be either a prediction by Jesus or an insertion after the martyrdom of James and John. But does the text really necessarily indicate this? It seems more probable that Jesus knew, in a way that the disciples could not at that point, that those who were closely associated with him could expect a fate similar to his.

Barratt goes on to cite:

(1) an epitomist of the historian Philip of Side (*c*.A.D. 430) that:
   "Papias in his second book says that John the Divine and James his brother were killed by the Jews".

(2) Georgius Monachus (9th century) gives an similar reference to Papias:
   "Papias, Bishop of Hieropolis, who was an eyewitness of him (sc. Of John), in the second book of the Oracles of the Lord, says that he was killed by the Jews".

(3) Two martyrologies, a Syriac *c*.A.D. 411 and The Calendar of Carthage (*c*.A.D. 505) which suggest that James and John were killed by the Jews.

II Analysis of the External Evidence

Now the time has come to evaluate the documents given above as to and what they have to tell us about the authorship of the Fourth Gospel. These will be considered one by one in the first instance to make clear what each one has to contribute and what it doesn't.

Irenaeus (see I, B for documents). Irenaeus says that John the Apostle is the source of the Fourth Gospel (HE 5. 8). It is of interest that as he lists the four Gospels, in the order we now have them, he writes "Matthew *published*"; "Mark, the disciple and interpreter of Peter, *transmitted*"; "Luke, the follower of Paul, *set down in a book*": "John, the disciple of the Lord, who had leant back on his breast, once more ('published' or 'set forth' or 'gave out') the Gospel while residing in Asia". Thus Irenaeus makes a distinction between the ways in which the four Gospels were produced. This will be important in our conclusions later.

Also very important for this study is the use of the phrase *"leant back upon his breast"* (H.E. 5. 8, see I, B above). This phrase is also used by Polycrates (see I, D above) but will be commented upon here. Brownlee[6] has this to say:

"The description of the beloved disciple as reclining in the bosom of Jesus means far more than a relationship of affection and intimacy, as is shown by

---

[6] Brownlee, quoted by J. A. Robinson in *The Priority of John from Brownlee* "Whence the Gospel of John in Charlesworth" ed. John and Qumran.

Jubilees 22:26 where 'Jacob slept in the bosom of Abraham'. This occurred when the older patriarch was about to die, but he first conferred his final blessing (along with much moral exhortation) on his grandson. Lying in the testator's bosom seems to designate one as the true son and heir. In Luke 16:19-23 it is Lazarus the poor beggar who lies in the patriarch's bosom. It was just like Jesus to show in this way that the social outcast rather than the rich man is the true son of Abraham. Jubilees 22:26 is in the context of Abraham's final blessing and testamentary exhortation. It is on a like occasion that the beloved disciple lies on Jesus' breast. This means that he and all true disciples (whom he symbolizes) inherit the task, the Spirit, and the peace which Jesus has bequeathed. Similarly, the divine Logos as God's only-begotten is one 'in the bosom of the Father' (1:18) for he is the heir of all things, to whom all that the Father has belongs (16:15).

This is important in two ways. First of all it has an importance in his use in the Gospel indicating the role of the Beloved Disciple as heir. But its use by Irenaeus and Polycrates can be seen to indicate their acceptance of this role for the Beloved Disciple and, as far as the Fourth Gospel is concerned, it implies a particular authority, i.e. the Fourth Gospel was written by one who was the designated heir of Jesus.

In addition to saying that John *produced* the fourth Gospel and his use of the phrase *"had leant back upon his breast"*, Ireneaus also says (HE 3: 23) that John, the Lord's disciple, remained in Ephesus until Trajan's time (A.D. 98), that he had oversight of the churches in Asia and that he taught them.

As evidence for these statements Irenaeus cites **Papias** and **Polycarp**. Papias (see I, A, above) is said by Irenaeus to have listened to John and having been a companion of Polycarp. Eusebius, however, corrects Irenaeus and says that Papias himself made no such claim that he had heard the apostle. Eusebius then goes on to quote Irenaeus quoting Papias. What Papias says in this passage is that he has been careful and discerning in his pursuit of the truth. Papias then goes on to give two lists. "And whenever anyone came who had been a follower of the presbyters, I inquired into the words of the presbyters, what Andrew or Peter *had said*, or Philip or Thomas or James or John or Matthew, or any other disciple of the Lord, and what Aristion and the presbyter John, disciples of the Lord *were still saying*". Then he goes on to say that he valued more verbal than written records.

Here is it worth noting two points: the first is that Papias gives in the two lists two men named John i.e. John the disciple and John the presbyter; the second point is that he indicates (from the tenses of the verb, *underlined* above) that the disciples were before his time but that Aristion and the Presbyter John were in his time. This puts Papias as an early witness to the verbal tradition, but it also raises some problems. If Papias were living in Hieropolis (about 100 miles from Ephesus) about the time that Irenaeus says John the disciple was in Ephesus why didn't he go to listen to John himself, especially as he so valued the words of those who had known Jesus in his ministry in Palestine. Papias is also cited by two later authors (see 1, F above) as the authority for a divergent tradition, that John died an (early?) martyrs death. If so, and the death is taken to be early, then he is giving contradictory evidence.

Polycarp (see I, C above for text) is also cited by Irenaeus as a person who was "instructed by the apostles and conversant with many who had seen the Lord" and that he "taught the things which he had learnt from the apostles". Furthermore, Irenaeus also describes in considerable detail how he himself, when he was a boy, had known Polycarp and he also describes very carefully how clear his recollections are of those days and why. In the account of Polycarp's martyrdom by burning, Polycarp says that he had served Christ 86 years so there is no reason to doubt that Irenaeus knew him personally. Irenaeus also tells us that Polycarp conversed with John.

Polycrates (see I, D above for text) mentions two saints who decorate Asia and who will rise at the Lord's advent, Philip the apostle and "John, who leant back on the Lord's breast, and who became a priest wearing the mitre, a martyr and a teacher; he too sleeps in Ephesus".

So Polycrates tells us that John, who leant back on the Lord's breast, was a priest, is buried in Ephesus. On the importance of the phrase, "leant back on the Lord's breast" see under Irenaeus above.

The Muratorian Canon (see I, E above for text). This document states that John is the author of the Fourth Gospel. It adds the interesting detail that John did not produce this Gospel on his own. Rather, after a three day fast, John and his fellow-disciples and bishops called to mind what was revealed to them and John wrote them down. Thus it was, according to this source, a joint effort. The document also attempts to explain differences in the Gospels and, it would seem in this context, between the synoptics and John.

Clement of Alexandria (see I, B above for text). Clement *c.*150-215 is cited, along with Irenaeus, as a reliable witness by Eusebius. Clement writes, in the portion quoted by Eusebius, that John the disciple moved from Patmos to Ephesus and that he had pastoral oversight in the area around Ephesus. Clement is writing later than the writers mentioned above.

Jerome (see I, F above for text). Jerome gives us an appealing vignette telling us that John lived to an extreme old age in Ephesus. The other interesting feature about this is that we are told that this John in his old age (dotage?) kept using the same expression, "Little children, love one another". This recalls both John 15: 12 ("love one another as I have loved you") and the repeated reference to the reader as "Little children" (I John 2:1, 12, 28 etc.).

Anti-Marcionite Prologue (see I, G above for text). Here we are told that the Gospel was "revealed" by John to the Church while "he was still in the body". It goes on to add the statement that Papias was John's amanuensis. Marcion could hardly have been rebuked by John, having died *c*.160.

III Comment on the above documentation.

Now let us assemble the picture that emerges of John the Apostle. This is most conveniently done in chart form (next page).

Suffice it to say at this stage that the documents cited show remarkably few contradictions and, given the fact that they come from a diversity of sources, a remarkable consistency. But the evidence has been subject to great scrutiny and it is necessary now to go on to consider how and on what grounds it has been attacked or dismissed.

IV Examination of External Evidence

It needs to be said at the outset that the attention paid to the evidence (1 above) has depended very much on the underlying assumptions of the critics. For instance, if is it held that Philo's Logos doctrine is a key to understanding the Fourth Gospel then there is a vested interest in downgrading the role of Ephesus (and John the apostle) and in building up the case by postulating Alexandria as the place of writing. If, on the other hand, the Fourth Gospel is seen as coming out of a primarily Jewish matrix, some have argued for this and other reasons that the place of writing is Antioch. This, too affects the consideration of the documentary evidence. Likewise if a Hellenistic background for the Fourth Gospel is regarded as a primary influence then Ephesus becomes a more likely location for writing and the evidence of Irenaeus *et al* is more important. Those who would have dated the authorship of the Gospel in the middle of the 2nd century must dismiss the documents purporting to show John as author (because of age) and Ephesus as location, and postulate a longer redactional period. Theological and critical considerations also affect the weight given to the early documentary evidence of authorship.

V Summary of External Evidence regarding John the Apostle and The Fourth Gospel

	Irenaeus	Papias	Polycarp	Clement of Alexandria	Polycrates	Muratorian Canon	Jerome	Anti-Marcionite Prologue to 4th
John source of the 4th Gospel						✔		✔ "revealed"
or worked with other	✔			"urged ✔ by friends"		✔		"Papias amanucnsis
"leant upon Jesus breast"	✔				✔			
John lived in Ephesus	✔		✔	✔	✔		✔	
Asia	✔							
John lived to an old age	✔ (To A.D.98)	(died as a martyr)	✔ conversed with John	✔ tale of "young man"			✔ "extreme old age"	✔
Additional information	John had oversight of churches	Papias heard 2nd generation of witnesses		John had pastoral oversight	John became priest	Offers explanation of differences in Gospels	John said, "Little children, love one another"	
Conflicting Evidence	Irenaeus says Papias heard John	Two sources quote Papias that John died a Martyr.						

✔ means implied rather than stated

A good illustration of this is Bultmann. He dismisses the above documents in a paragraph. He believes that "we are not in a position to say anything definite about the author or about the redactor", although he grants that the redactor holds the author to be an eyewitness. He is worth quoting further not only because he illustrates how critical perspectives influence the weighting of the external documentation but because he offers a good (and succinct!) starting point for our consideration of that documentation. Bultmann writes[7] "Later the Beloved Disciple was equated with John, the Son of Zebedee and brother of

---

[7] Bultmann, R., *The Gospel of John*, page 11.

James, a member of the circle of the Twelve, and it was claimed that he died in advanced age in Ephesus. The first clear testimony to this tradition is offered by Irenaeus III. 1-2 *But John the son of Zebedee must have been killed by the Jews very early, as Mk. 10:39 shows and as is indicated by several witnesses of the ancient Church.* Moreover, the Gospel itself makes no claim to have been written by an eyewitness. (Bultmann regards John 21 as a redactional appendix). And in no way does it give occasion to presume that an eyewitness lies behind it, rather it completely contradicts such an assumption.[8]

Bultmann continues: "Now the much discussed testimony of Papias (in Eusebius H.E. III. 39. 3f) refers not only to John the son of Zebedee but also to the Presbyter John, who may have written the Book of Revelation. Probably Irenaeus and the whole later tradition confused the Ephesian Presbyter with the son of Zebedee of the same name. Prior to Irenaeus, then, the Presbyter John could have been regarded as the author of the Fourth Gospel and possibly this was already the view of the redactor of the Gospel. But this assumption, of course, is quite uncertain, and it is no longer possible to demonstrate the correctness of such an opinion. The author remains unknown to us".

The point to be made here is that Bultmann has decided, on the basis of his *internal* examination of the Gospel, that the author is unknown and so dismisses the *external* evidence about authorship in a pre-emptory fashion, regarding it as largely superfluous. Thus his consideration of the external evidence has been very much conditioned by these assumptions.

But to go back to Bultmann in a different way and use him as a beginning for our consideration of the external evidence, he says in the first paragraph quoted above that "John the son of Zebedee must have been killed by the Jews very early, as Mark 10:39 shows, and as is indicated by several witnesses of the ancient Church". Mark 10:38-9 and the "several ancient witnesses" are summarized under 'I. H. Other Evidence' above. As commented there, Mark 10:38-9 might be capable of Bultmann's interpretation, among others far more likely, but certainly cannot be held to "show" conclusively that James and John suffered an early martyr's death. This is the verdict of recent commentators. Furthermore, in regard to the "several ancient witnesses" (cited under I, G above), we are faced with a stark choice between earlier and detailed accounts by Irenaeus and Eusebius whose accuracy has been demonstrated in other ways and such as Philip of Side and Georgius Monachus who wrote later and who are not accurate historians. Barratt[9] expresses the consensus when he writes:

---

[8] Bultmann, *ibid.*
[9] Barrett, *The Gospel According to John* (2nd Edition).

"In fact we are almost compelled to choose between the veracity of Irenaeus and Eusebius on the one hand and the intelligence and accuracy of Philip and George on the other. It is a comparison which does credit to the earlier writers. If, however, Philip and George are discredited, the other evidence falls to the ground". This seems a balanced and fair assessment.

Going on further with Bultmann, in the second paragraph quoted above he mentions that Papias refers to the two Johns and then Bultmann presumes that Irenaeus and the whole later tradition confused the Presbyter John with the Apostle. Thus, his argument goes, Presbyter John could have been regarded as the author of the Fourth Gospel by those prior to Irenaeus and possibly by the redactor of the Gospel. Let us examine this, starting with Papias. The contrary argument, that is, in favour of Papias knowing and meaning what he wrote, is based upon these considerations.

(1) Papias (see I, A above) says of himself that "in days gone by I carefully learnt from the presbyters and have carefully recalled, for I can guarantee its truth". This doesn't mean that he did what he intended but his intention is worth noting.

(2) He appears to have carefully differentiated between the two lists of apostles and presbyters. Hengel[10] makes the point of the similarity between the order of Papias' list of apostles (Andrew, Peter, Philip, Thomas, James, John and Matthew) and that in John (1:40 and 21:2). This argument could be used both ways (i.e. as a careless use of a usual ordering, or as a confirmation of proximity to the author) but it is hard to imagine that Papias would be confused as to two Johns. He was close in time to either or both Johns and it would have been a grave abuse of his stated purpose to have been careless in this way.

(3) But the change in tenses of verbs (already noted in 2 above) seems to be conclusive. Papias refers to what the apostles "had said" and what Aristion and the presbyter John "were saying". By making this differentiation he shows care in distinguishing his generation from the one preceding, i.e. those whose testimony he had received secondhand and those he had heard himself.

For these reasons it seems there is no outstanding reason to doubt Papias' account. But what of the other main strands of evidence? Eusebius, although regarded as the Father of Church History, was not above suppressing information he found distasteful. We have only fragments of Papias' work but Eusebius and Irenaeus had read the whole. If Papias had listened to the presbyter John would there not have been other or more specific references? We have noted how Irenaeus was corrected by Eusebius when he said Papias had

---

[10] Martin Hengel, *The Johannine Question*, pages 17-18.

listened to John. Irenaeus also says that Polycarp and Papias knew each other and that this is questionable. If Irenaeus went beyond his sure information in this instance how reliable was he in the main? Irenaeus was certainly concerned to show that John lived in Ephesus and produced the Fourth Gospel. Did he shape a tradition to give credence to his concern. No final answers can be given to these questions but the writings of both Eusebius and Irenaeus are greatly respected for different reasons and once again, it would seem that there does not exist sufficient reason to doubt what they say. Irenaeus' moving account of hearing Polycarp as a boy has the ring of truth; Eusebius is generally reliable. It has been suggested that Polycrates made a mistake when he spoke of Philip the Apostle. If this is so, and there are other explanations, does it really make worthless what he says about John?

More important than some of the above is in the argument from silence. If John had lived in Ephesus to an old age and was the author of the Fourth Gospel and the Beloved Disciple, would this not have been well-known in the early second century and referred to by others whose silence has been noted? This is a sound question. There may be another answer to it, consistent with the thesis of the book, and this will be given in the conclusion following.

VI Conclusion: External Evidence

It is the conclusion of this chapter that there exists no reason to doubt the documentary evidence, individually or collectively, if taken by itself. It is recognized that, in practice, this is difficult, that our theological and critical attitudes, influenced particularly by our analysis as to the internal evidence of the Gospel, and such matters as our position on the authorship of the Gospel vis-à-vis the Epistles vis-à-vis Revelation, are bound to affect how we evaluate the documents. This inherent difficulty is exacerbated by the fact that there isn't as much there as we might expect or have hoped for, and complicated by the very name of John (the possibility of two Johns in Ephesus and more than one involved in producing Gospel/Epistles/Revelation). Thus what is there is more susceptible to being dismissed as being unimportant, irrelevent or mistaken. Nonetheless, it is held here that if the evidence is examined impartially it holds together to present a consistent albeit thin picture. This is true and especially noteworthy in that the evidence has been subjected to great scrutiny almost since it has been written and particularly in the last two centuries.

So first of all, what is that consistent picture? (see chart, above, III, for easy reference). It is that John the apostle, son of Zebedee, lived in Ephesus to an old age and that he *produced* the Fourth Gospel in conjunction with others. A glance at the chart supports this. Five of the sources listed put John in Ephesus.

Irenaeus states that John lived to the time of Trajan (A.D. 98) but three others imply that he lived to an old age. Three agree that he was the source of the Gospel but say or imply that he worked with assistance of others. Two make the additional claim that John was the "one who leant upon Jesus' breast", the Beloved Disciple. The importance of this phrase as indicating a special relationship with Jesus and authority for the Fourth Gospel has been suggested (see II, Irenaeus, above).

Analysis of the evidence is not primarily a statistical exercise, the documents vary in the time they were written and in their general accuracy and reliability. The information given is piecemeal in that it comes from a variety of sources, most of which only contribute a fact or two. In a way, that makes a stronger case. But it is remarkable in that there is very little contradictory evidence. The only important instance of this is the claim that John died an early death. But the evidence for that has been shown as being comparatively unsubstantial. Additional detail is supplied by some sources, some of it doubtful (e.g. that Papias heard John, that Papias was John's amanuensis), some of it of interest (e.g. that John was a priest, that he exercised pastor oversight in Asia).

Now it remains to go back to the question posed above. If John lived to an old age in Ephesus and was the author of the Gospel, why wasn't more known and written and earlier? This is especially true in that the Fourth Gospel is now thought to have been written A.D. 90-100 and to be the latest[11] of the Gospels. Whereas the synoptics were written earlier and might have undergone a somewhat different process of evolution which has obscured the details of authorship, John is thought to have been written later. Add to this the somewhat controversial nature of the Fourth Gospel, that it was used first by gnostics perhaps because they, mistakenly, thought it supported their theology. Taking these factors together we would have thought that the apostolic authorship of the Gospel would have been more thoroughly investigated and commented on in the second century A.D. What is the answer to this question?

The answer that this study proposes is that the partial obscurity surrounding the Fourth Gospel's origin was deliberate and, indeed, necessary. That is, that just as the author/redactor put the mysterious Beloved Disciple figure in the text of the Gospel deliberately and out of sheer necessity, so it was necessary to blur the picture as to who was the source when the Gospel was first circulated. The identity of the eyewitness source of the Gospel could not be disclosed because his own character was fatally flawed and, if known, might have discredited that Gospel itself. Judas/Beloved Disciple needed the highest authority possible i.e.

---

[11] J. A. T. Robinson, *The Priority of John*, presenting an important alternative.

apostolic authority for his work, not only because of his own background but because he, at points, gave a different account from that of the synoptics. John the apostle gave his authority to the Fourth Gospel, being convinced of its value by his own experience as a disciple, by its intrinsic merit (as so many have been down through the centuries) as well perhaps as by the sincere marks of repentance and change he saw in Judas. But John and Judas couldn't just credit the Gospel to John, full stop. First of all it wasn't true (and this Gospel presents Christ as truth and emphasizes the role of the Spirit of truth). Secondly, it is likely that by the time Judas came to John enough was known about John by his contemporaries during his long stay and ministry in Ephesus as to make it unlikely that he, unaided, could have produced the Gospel (e.g. that he wrote in a different style, or was the author of Revelation, or couldn't write at all, or was decrepit). It was necessary to confuse, or fuse, the identities of John the apostle and the Beloved Disciple/Judas. This may even have been a bit of deliberate misinformation or a case where certain facts were added up to a wrong conclusion.

So, the Gospel was circulated to a limited group, at first. It was made known that John took overall responsibility (as he did) but that he had worked in conjunction with others (which he had). This doesn't preclude the possibility that John took an active part in the compiling, perhaps even contributing a major element like the discourses in the Upper Room. It doesn't necessarily preclude the existence of a Johannine Community as is now thought likely by some. This theory helps to provide an explanation for some other perplexing problems (e.g. that of the similarities/dissimilarities between Gospel/Epistles/Revelation.

So, the point to be made in this chapter is that the evidence we have from the early Church Fathers, thin as it is, nonetheless presents a consistent, accurate, reliable and, so far as it goes, an informative account of the position in regard to authorship, and that even the paucity of material was deliberate and necessary

Chapter VII

Brief Academic History and Background

Through the years, this thesis in manuscript form has been submitted to outstanding Biblical scholars with worldwide reputations. They have asked searching and critical questions. The book has benefitted greatly from their scrutiny. Their suggestions have been incorporated into the book you are now reading. In the main these scholars have been supportive and encouraging.

Until Raymond E. Brown produced his magisterial work on *The Gospel According to St John*, students of the Fourth Gospel, following Rudolph Bultmann, commonly rejected the idea that the Fourth Gospel was written by one man; they were occupied in finding multiple sources which had been worked over by redactors. Bultmann found three sources; one of his students six; and others ultimately found up to 50 different sources. In addition, the Fourth Gospel (vis-a-vis the Synoptics), was not thought to have much historical value, or value in reconstructing the life of Jesus. In this academic atmosphere, it was thought naïve to believe, as B. F. Westcott argued with considerable erudition in the 19th century, that the Fourth Gospel was written by one man. If the Gospel were worked over by 50 different redactors or had that many sources and was not a reliable source of material about the life and ministry of Jesus, than any investigation into the identity of the Beloved Disciple was irrelevant. Who could possibly guess on what basis and what difference could it make?

Nonetheless, I sent my work to Professor Charles Moule, Cambridge University, Bishop John A. T. Robinson (Cambridge University), Lord Blanch, Professor Brevard Childs (Yale University) and others. Each of these was an outstanding Biblical scholar. Each of them was encouraging. None of them "bought" my theory in its entirety but none of them thought it was preposterous. Each took the time to write a careful and helpful critique. Stuart Blanch, when Archbishop of York, suggested several publishers. Lord Blanch's Domestic Chaplain wrote on his behalf in a letter of 23 September 1982. "He would be quite happy to be quoted as saying that while not necessarily agreeing with the conclusions of your study, he believes the publication should stimulate the thinking of any who are interested in the authorship of St. John." He found my analysis of the internal evidence (the heart of my study) "convincing".

Dr Matt Melko, said that he was "surprised by the venom with which my thesis was rejected". We don't readily give up our Judas stereotype, the man the world loves to hate.

The Johannine academic atmosphere changed with the publication of R. E. Brown's *Commentary*. In the Introduction, in his usual closely reasoned and very thorough manner, he gives a comprehensive summary of the evidence and presents the theories or aspects of Johannine authorship. Once more it was academically respectable to hold that the Fourth Gospel could have been written by "**a** towering theologian", and that it contained useful historical information. As Brown shows, scholars came to think that the Fourth Gospel rivals Matthew in providing historical information. Further, Brown's "guess" is that the first edition might have been as early as A.D. 70-85. It follows that the identity of the Beloved Disciple is a legitimate question and that this study is back in business. I am clearly indebted to the thorough work Brown has done on the Fourth Gospel.

After presenting in detail the ideas and theories of others, Brown presents his own ideas on the authorship of the Fourth Gospel. He posits five stages in the composition of the Fourth Gospel.

Three major studies having a major influence on *Judas, Beloved Disciple*

The Gospel According to John
A New Translation with Introduction and Commentary
By Raymond E. Brown
1966

Brown's 5 stages follow with his page numbers in (brackets). The way in which the thesis of this book fits neatly into Brown's five stages are indicated by *italics*.

"Stage 1 (page xxxiv): "The existence of a body of traditional material pertaining to the works and words of Jesus – material similar to what has gone into the Synoptic Gospels but material which is independent of the Synoptic tradition."

Brown wrote, before the discovery of **The Judas Gospel,** *(reported in the May* **2006** *National Geographic). "The Judas Gospel may be the "traditional material" which was known to Irenaeus and was the raison d'etre of a first century 'Judas community'. Fragments exist of the Egerton Gospel, dating from the 2nd century. The Jesus Seminar Fellows call this "Egerton" and believe it was a source for the Fourth Gospel, as well as the 'Signs'."*

"The Judas Gospel and the Egerton fragment may well be, in modern parlance, a floater, an early draft of the Fourth Gospel purposely and anonymously floated to see how the Christian community would react. The Signs were from another source."
It is worth mentioning in passing that Brown raises the question here of "whether or not the material (i.e. in this stage) came from an *eye witness*". This is interesting in the light of what Bauckham writes decades later. *The pieces of the puzzle fall into place.*

"Stage 2 (pages xxxiv and xxxv). The development of the material in Johannine patterns. Over a period lasting perhaps several decades, the material was sifted, selected, thought over and moulded into the form or style" . . . "that became the Fourth Gospel". . . . "This was probably accomplished through oral teaching and preaching". . . . "That this preaching and teaching was the work of **more than one** man is suggested by units of material that are different in style" . . . "we should think of a close knit school of thought and expression." *The "more than one man" are, in my theory, the Beloved Disciple, and John the apostle/ (John* *the Elder of Ephesus); they would have had very different lives since the crucifixion. I believe the Beloved Disciple had to escape into the wilderness and spent long periods in isolation. John of Ephesus was, on the other hand, the centre of a community. Their very different lives account for different styles and vocabulary.*

"Stage 3 (pages xxxv and xxvi). The organization of the material from stage 2 into a consecutive Gospel. *This was done in lengthy consultations between two people: the Beloved Disciple and the Apostle John. The consultations had to be secret so no one would guess the identity of the Beloved Disciple. John and the Beloved Disciple shared the same experiences in the band of 12 disciples and they would have cross checked their memories to sort out the chronology, and other matters.*

"Stage 4 (page xxxvi). Secondary edition by the evangelist. It is possible that the evangelist edited his Gospel several times" . . . "but most of the features that seem to require a second editing can be explained in terms of **one** re-editing" *So much for mulitple redactors, the fashion at the time Brown was writing.*

"Stage 5 (pages xxxvi and xxxxvii). A final editing or redaction by someone other than the evangelist and whom we shall call the redactor We think that the most likely supposition is that the redactor was a close friend or **disciple** of the evangelist and certainly part of the general school of thought to which we referred in Stage 2."

The supposition of my study is that the last three stages happened this way. The apostle John had gathered around him a community of disciples. The Beloved Disciple made cautious contact and the two got together, without others being present They "sifted, selected, thought over and moulded" *their memories and experiences of the words and works of Jesus. The Beloved Disciple made his contribution, his memories; John his. These were overlapping, sometimes they had both been present, sometimes not. Memory is curious. An old person may have vivid, precise and accurate memories of events, words and actions, body language and photographic images of things that happened decades ago. The two disciples had much to share; they had both been powerfully affected by Jesus; they were eyewitnesses. They spent as much time as it took, reminiscing and working carefully over the documents available-see John 21.25. They assembled their material in some way, perhaps not even in documentary form. If not, they dictated to an amanuensis. This was an especially trustworthy member of John's community, trusted with the knowledge that the hitherto unknown stranger John had been spending so much time with, was a Beloved Disciple. They reworked their document and asked other members of the community to proof read the final document, our Fourth Gospel. This process is similar but different to what happened with the synoptics. This difference accounts for the often remarked distinctive style of the Fourth Gospel.*

Now we leave Brown. In his 5 stage hypothesis, the last stages have been amalgamated; but the process is the same. What is written in italics can't be proven but it is, at the least possible, and, I believe, probably, much the way the Fourth Gospel came into being. The Fourth Gospel was then "released" as "The Gospel according to John".

The Five Gospels
The Search for the Authentic Words of Jesus
New Translation and Commentary
By Robert W. Funk
Roy W. Hoover
And The Jesus Seminar
1997

The Jesus Seminar was a blockbuster, the blocks busted being our ecclesiastical mindsets in the way of critical, free, open minded and untrammelled interpretation of the Gospels. But, as I argue below, there may be other blocks that even groups of Biblical scholars are subject to, but unaware of. Votes do not necessarily produce truth. The process the Jesus Seminar followed was disciplined, involved and time consuming. They assembled and, after individual study, divided into groups and subgroups, went into plenary session for discussion and finally voted on various issues including each place where Jesus was quoted to have spoken, in all four of the Gospels. They then produced their translation (SV) in four coded colours. The Jesus Seminar, by the process of voting, concluded that 82% of the words purported to be spoken by Jesus had not actually been spoken by him. Fundamentalists of all types went on the attack with missionary zeal. Was this just another kooky idea to come out of California? Unappreciated were the linguistic and academic qualifications, the dedication, the erudition and faith of this odd and highly unusual, broadly interdenominational, international grouping of 100 scholars, Fellows and associates. The Jesus Seminar is also a magisterial work. Among many other matters it gives an accurate and useful summary of the history of biblical criticism. A sample nugget (Page 2) is that Thomas Jefferson (1743-1826) "scrutinized the Gospels" . . . "to separate the real teachings of Jesus". Importantly, The Jesus Seminar revived for our generation, the search for the Jesus of history.

Of particular interest to this study is the following:

"The Fellows of the Seminar have been unable to find a single saying (in John's Gospel) that they could in certainty trace back to the historical Jesus" (page 10).

They do, however, print in **black** the I AM sayings in John (page 419). They also print in **black**, (on a scale from red to pink to grey to black, red being words ascribed to Jesus and black "inauthentic") the words in Chapter 21. This chapter contains John's final resurrection scene. Chapter 21 is crucial to my study. Here the resurrected Jesus is depicted in a wraithlike or ghostly way. Christian comment about the mystery of the resurrection has swirled around since it was first experienced, depending on the commentators' base point (i.e. theology, opinion or mindset). Westcott suggested the word "mystical" as conveying the physical and spiritual aspects of resurrection. The point here is not to argue how Jesus was present. I have presented my view elsewhere. But the point of this study is that even if these words in John 21 are rated "inauthentic" words of Jesus (as they are) but are printed in **black**, could this not indicate some doubt? And might the Jesus Seminar Fellows' objectivity on these particular words been influenced by their different views of the resurrection? i.e. some might have been inclined to reject these as authentic words of Jesus because they believe Jesus was not physically present, or the reverse, so he could hardly have spoken the words in Chapter 21. The Jesus Seminar Fellows have pointed out how our ecclesiastical and theological mindset can distort our perceptions. Such distortion not only relates to individuals but might it also be manifest in the social dynamics of a group. In any case, they allow the possibility, albeit remote, that the words in Chapter 21 (John's epilogue) might possibly be the words of Jesus. The Epilogue is of great importance to this study because: this was the occasion when the Beloved Disciple is referred to as "the disciple whom Jesus loved *most*", in the Jesus Seminar translation (*an interesting "most", which covers a lot of ground)!* This is important because it is in Chapter 21 that the Beloved Disciple claims he is an eyewitness and claims to be the originator of the 4th Gospel.

Turning to the historicity of Chapter 21, the Fellows argue that the placement of the Fishing and Breakfast on the shore in John 21.1-14 is more likely than that in Luke (5:1-11). This is remarkable in that, following traditional critical theory, the Fellows rate the Synoptics higher in historicity than the 4th Gospel. Note that (pages 14-17): The Jesus Seminar do rate John as an independent source (among Mark, Q, Mt., Luke, Thomas and Egerton. They also, with Brown, believe the 4th Gospel was "produced by a school of disciples" (box, page 20).

Pursuing this line of thought, The Jesus Seminar say (page 10):

"In the synoptic gospels, Jesus speaks in brief, pithy one-liners and couplets, and in parables. In John, by contrast, Jesus speaks in lengthy discourses or monologues or in elaborate dialogues."

There is this difference, most marked in John 13-17 (substantially different in style from the rest of the book). But in the other chapters there are in John dialogues, exchanges and conversations which have all the hallmarks of real conversations, with Jesus interactive with various individuals and groups. These occur throughout the 4th Gospel and have been oft commented on.

However, if you start with the scholarly conviction that the Synoptics are the earlier and more accurate record (the verdict of most scholars) might not even the Jesus Seminar Fellows have turned this on its head and down rated the verdict of Johannine scholars that John gives important historical information? It would be interesting to know how many of the 100 were specifically Johannine scholars. Might the vote have been skewed?

My argument has been that the tools (well delineated on page 2-4, "The Seven Pillars of Scholarly Wisdom" (note at the beginning of a book of over 500 pages) which have served so well in analyzing other parts of the Bible, including the Old Testament and the Synoptics, have to be used with extreme discretion in approaching the 4th Gospel which is another animal, no matter how you look at it.

So, I conclude that although in general terms, the conclusions of the Jesus Seminar might seem to be destructive of my thesis, nonetheless there is encouragement also. In particular, in the crucial, to my study, Chapter 21, I believe the Fellows give evidence valuable to my study in their translation and in their evaluation of the historicity of John.

Jesus and the Eyewitnesses
The Gospels as Eyewitness Testimony
By Richard Bauckham
2006

Richard Bauckham received the Michael Ramsay Prize for Theological Writing at the 2009 Hays Festival of Literature and Arts. There are prizes and prizes, but **this** prize was presented by an Archbishop who is a noted theologian himself; his wife is also a theologian.

Richard Bauckham's book is another blockbuster; the blocks in this case are those noted above in the analysis of the *Five Gospels* – mainly the sub-conscious?

mindset of the Jesus Fellows in applying, to the Fourth Gospel, without "**due discretion**", the same critical tools of form criticism that have served Biblical scholarship so well in analyzing the Old Testament, the Epistles in the New Testament and the Synoptic Gospels. But these tools don't deal with the real situation, sitz im Leben (life setting), in the Fourth Gospel. Bauckham refers to this at the outset (page 7). In his references to form criticism he describes Vincent Taylor, as "the scholar who did the most to introduce the methods of German form criticism into English speaking New Testament scholarship"; and, in support, quotes him on form criticism. He goes on – "More recently Martin Hengel has insisted, against the form critical approach, that the personal link of the Jesus tradition with particular tradents, or more precisely their memory and missionary preaching . . . is undeniable". Bauckham goes on to say that; "The Gospels were written within living memory of the events they recount. . . . But the period in question is actually that of a relatively (for that period) long lifetime". This gives credence to my ideas about the reunion in old age of the Beloved Disciple and John the Apostle, whom Bauckham believes is John the Elder of Ephesus.

Bauckham gives impressive and convincing scholarly evidence of the validity and the importance of the Eyewitness accounts of the Jesus of history. He enumerates and analyzes these in detail. Of particular importance to my study, he refers frequently and at great length to the Beloved Disciple. A whole chapter, out of 18, is entitled, *The Witness of the Beloved Disciple* (page 364 ff). In terms of volume, 3 chapters, out of 18, 58 pages, out of 525, are exclusively devoted to the Fourth Gospel. Most of the other material mentions, sometimes at length, the Fourth Gospel and/or the Beloved Disciple. He sees the Beloved Disciple as a prime example of an eyewitness in the mode of what he identifies as one whose testimony embodies that of other eyewitnesses ("*inclusio*").

He summarizes his conclusions to page 384 as:

"We have demonstrated that according to John 21.24, the Beloved Disciple was both the primary witness on whose testimony the Gospel is based and also himself the author of the Gospel".

In terms of memory, he has another chapter – Eyewitness *Memory* (Chap 18), in which he gives added weight to memory and oral tradition. He points out that the Gospels were written within living memory of eyewitnesses, if they lived to an old age for their time. This is an important plank in my analysis. It has oft been noted that old people can remember the past when they can't call to mind instantly, shorter term memories. So their memories cannot be faulted even if they can't remember their own phone numbers. Bauckham's comments on memory and oral tradition are corroborated by the alpinist, Mortenson, (see my Bibliography) who found that residents of an isolated Himalayan village remembered in story/song (a common way of remembering) (cf. the Old Testament, Luke's Gospel) the coming of Alexander the Great to their area 2300 years earlier. Oral tradition is not to be lightly dismissed! It can be very accurate in detail. As I have commented otherwise, one tribe in Uganda, with no reference to written records which hadn't existed, could recite from memory the full names of their ancestors going back over 20 generations, collateral and direct, hundreds or thousands of people. In the OT period business transactions were conducted without permanent written records, but were held in the memories of transactors.

Bauckham's work as a whole gives new life to my study. He believes that John was the author (KATA) of the Fourth Gospel. This is the verdict of history, and one which I support with the important caveat that it was a joint venture with the Beloved Disciple and John's community. This fits neatly into Brown's 5 stage process.

Bauckham is in the mainstream of British scholarship from before, and after, Bishop Westcott, who wrote (1890), what is still the best commentary in English on the Gospel of John. It is great to see British scholarly common sense winning prizes.

CONCLUSION

As I believe and have written, it is plausible albeit arguable to believe that the Beloved Disciple made contact with the John the Apostle when they were both old men. Together, and in secret, they worked on a Gospel, enlisting the help of John's community. This produced our Fourth Gospel. For a while it seemed as though Jesus Fellows' analysis: "we have not been able to find a single saying in St. John's Gospel, that we could in certainty trace back to the historical Jesus" appeared to destroy my thesis. I think that I have written enough to indicate some doubt about this. In particular, I argue that the conversations Jesus had with Nicodemus (John 3: 1-15), with others, and with Peter (John 21:15-23) have all the hallmarks of authenticity in the very believable give and take in the conversations. I would like to see the textural evidence on which the Jesus Seminar concluded that Jesus didn't say what he is purported to have said although I can hardly argue in detail with their group decision. If the Jesus Seminar results can be seen as destroying my thesis, which is based on the detailed analysis of the words of Jesus and the Beloved Disciple, then Amen. But the Jesus Seminar results also can equally be seen as negating some of the greatest commentaries on the Fourth Gospel – Westcott, Bultmann?, Robinson,

Temple, Brown and how many hundred others over 20 centuries? I doubt that "we can even begin to count them". (cf. John 21:25) Amen.

Even if Jesus didn't utter one word, or saying, attributed to him in the Fourth Gospel (as the Jesus Fellows), my analysis of the role of the Beloved Disciple is based as much on "situational analysis" and still valid. By "situational analysis", I mean the site, who is there?, and how are they grouped? What is the juxtaposition? Jesus Seminar gives credence to the historicity of the Fourth Gospel. The Beloved Disciple is present in the Upper Room where he washes *the disciples'* feet (John 13: 21-30); at the foot of the cross (John 19: 25-27) with *the three named women,* including *Mary, his mother*; at the empty tomb (John: 20:1-10) with *Peter* and *Mary;* by the Sea of Tiberias (John: 21) with *seven other disciples, including Peter. The italics above indicate "inclusio", where the Beloved Disciples' witness "includes" or embodies, that of the others. "Situational Analysis" in each of the four main incidents, tells us much.*

Finally, my overall conclusion is that these three books, the giants of late 20th and early 21st century scholarship, give substance to my thesis (Brown and Bauckham), or can be seen as making it to be at least plausible and arguable (the Jesus Seminar).

Chapter VIII

The Judas Gospel

National Geographic Magazine May 2006
By Andrew Cockburn. Photographs by Kenneth Garrett

This article tells of the recent recovery and discovery of a long lost document "copied in the third or fourth century from a second century original". "The *National Geographic* commissioned a top carbon dating laboratory at the University of Arizona to analyze the papyrus book, or codex, containing the gospel. Tests on five separate samples from the papyrus and the leather binding date the codex to sometime between A.D. 220 and 300." The Judas Gospel has caused a seismic shock among New Testament scholars. It has caused a re-evaluation of the place of Judas and, I believe, is another bit of evidence to test against my working hypothesis in Chapter I. The following are from the article on The Judas Gospel with actual *quotes from the Gospel in italics*. At the time of writing, the text is still being assembled, translated and analyzed by scholars.

What we have in the May 2006 *National Geographical* articles is as follows: The opening line of the first page reads," *the secret account of the revelation that Jesus spoke in conversation with Judas Iscariot . . .*" This "is a passage where Jesus is explaining to the disciples that they are on the wrong track". "The secret account gives us a very different Judas (than the four Gospels)." "In this version, he is a hero. Unlike the other disciples, he understands Christ's message. In handing Jesus over to the authorities, he is doing his leader's bidding, knowing full well the fate he will bring on himself. Jesus warns him:

"You will be cursed."

"The key passage comes when Jesus tells Judas that: *You will sacrifice the man that clothes me.*" "In plain English, Judas is going to kill Jesus – and do him a favour."

"That Judas is entrusted with this task is a sign of his special status. '*Lift up your eyes and look at the cloud and the light within and the stars surrounding.*'

Jesus tells him encouragingly, "*The star that leads the way is your star.*"

Much of this resonates with what we read in the four gospels. The Judas of *The Judas Gospel* is **not** completely different from the Judas of the four canonical gospels. They can be reconciled. In The Judas Gospel, the portrait of Judas and the interpretation seem self serving. There is no compelling reason to believe that it didn't originate with Judas. It could have been, as I postulate in Chapter I, a float, or a leak, or a launch, posted in an early Christian community where it would be copied, passed on, re-copied and circulated. We will never be certain. The author may have wanted to see how it would, if it would, be received. Would it provoke an orgy of papyrus destruction in the mode of the burning of The Satanic Verses? What would be the effect of the attribution to Judas?

What is certain is that Irenaeus in A.D. 180 knew of a Gospel and called it "fictitious history". We do not know whether this *National Geographic Judas Gospel* is the one Irenaeus knew but it is becoming more likely the closer we look at it. The dates check out reasonably well. Irenaeus know about it in A.D. 180; it could have been in circulation for a decade or so before it came to his attention. The crucifixion is dated to A.D. 30. Dating of St. John's Gospel has moved from c.A.D. 150 to as early as A.D. 120 to A.D. 90 to A.D. 80. So, going off the dates, it is possible, as I conjecture in Chapter II, that Judas spent some time in the wilderness and, at the end of this period, produced and 'floated' as a 'trial balloon' this *National Geographic The Judas Gospel*; he then went on, with St. John's help, to produce the Fourth Gospel, as I postulate in Chapter II. If Judas had been about the same age as Jesus, he could have been 50 to 70 when he wrote his Gospel. This is at the least possible.

The fact that the Fourth Gospel is thought to have been written down later than the synoptics doesn't necessarily mean that it is less reliable. Judas and John would both have been working on the Gospel when they were middle-aged or elderly. Age does not diminish the accuracy of long-term memory; a 90 year old veteran of WWI remembers with clarity and even photographic images events 70 years earlier. Similarly, contact with "The Word made Flesh" would have left an indelible impression on those who knew him in the flesh. On the other hand, the synoptics were worked over by redactors, some of whom hadn't known Jesus in the flesh and so they have most aspects of "a camel is a horse designed by a committee". Harpur* and the Jesus Seminar school believe that only a small part of the words in the Gospels, attributed to Jesus, were actually spoken by him. I argue that, if true, it is far more so of the synoptics than of the Fourth Gospel for the reason the latter was written or edited by one or two persons. Oral tradition, or folk memory, can be amazingly long-term and

* Tom Harpur *The Pagan Christ* Tom Harpur *Water Into Wine*

accurate. Mortenson** writes of a village in northern Pakistan, so remote it wasn't on any map of the region, who celebrated in song and story the coming of Alexander the Great to their region 23 centuries before. It is not uncommon for Africans and other cultures which don't have written records, to have memorized their ancestors 25 generations back.

In summary, the discovery of *The Judas Gospel* adds credibility to my hypothesis, that Judas, Beloved Disciple was the principle source of the Fourth Gospel and St. John was the editor, with his community of disciples helping in the final stages.

The Importance of *The Judas Gospel*

Judas is presented in *The Judas Gospel* differently than in the Gospels of Matthew, Mark and Luke but there are very significant and interesting similarities with the Fourth Gospel. In the May 2006 *National Geographic* article, *The Judas Gospel*, Judas is seen as doing Jesus' bidding in his betrayal "handing Jesus over to the authorities," and even in sacrificing (killing) Jesus. Compare this to the Fourth Gospel presentation of Judas and, particularly in John, Chapter 13.

"And during supper, when the devil had already put it into the heart of Judas Iscariot, Simon's son, to betray him" John 13.2

and

(after giving Judas the sop, and so making known to Judas that Jesus knew he was the betrayer, "Jesus said to him (Judas) what you are going to do, do quickly."

Both presentations, the Fourth Gospel and *The Judas Gospel* are self serving in different ways. In *The Judas Gospel*, Jesus commands Judas. In the Fourth Gospel (Chapter 13), Judas is told to do what the devil has put into his heart. Judas may have felt before and after than he had no choice; "the devil did it", an easy explanation for humans who sin. In any case, betrayal and crucifixion followed.

The *National Geographic* translator concludes that in *The Judas Gospel* presentation, Judas is seen as a "hero", the one who understands Jesus. This is not the case in the Fourth Gospel where Judas is presented "warts and all" but by then the author had had time to ponder.

These similarities, as well as the dissimilarities, are some, of many, indications that *The Judas Gospel* and the Fourth Gospel are by the same hand!

** Greg Mortenson and David Oliver Relin *Three Cups of Tea.*

Postscript

Or

How It All Came About

So here it is. I first had these ideas 50 years ago when I went to Christ Episcopal Church, Bethany, CT., U.S.A. as the first minister since the 1930s. It was a wonderful congregation, small and critical, but kind to their young deacon, later priest. I was expected to produce a sermon every Sunday; I had strong convictions about two subjects that were of great importance in the 1960s (Martin Luther King's Civil Rights Movement and Viet Nam). Initially, I welcomed the opportunity of presenting these in the pulpit. But week after week, on Monday and having a sermon in mind, I would read the appointed Gospel for the next Sunday and then throw out my prepared text because the words and ministry of Jesus were so much more exciting and important and relevant. I found other ways to let people know about my political opinions.

On one of these Monday mornings, I was preparing a sermon on St. John's account of what happened in the Upper Room. An idea occurred to me; it was completely absurd. It didn't appear in that week's sermon, that year or the next or the next, but it wouldn't go away. Years went by, the idea persisted as I studied other sections where the Beloved Disciple was mentioned. Still, I held off, uncertain. But then I took a two week sabbatical from my parish duties and went away to study, research and write; years later another two weeks off, a sabbatical in Uganda when Bishop Ruhindi found me a bolt hole, arranged for me to take a week out at the end of a very busy visit to write. Judas began to resemble a beaver's dam, bits added through the years (US, UK, Canada, Uganda, Nigeria) and so on and on. I sent the text to two of the greatest New Testament scholars, John Robinson and Charles Moule, both lecturing at Cambridge University when I was at Westcott House Theological College in 1955-56. I sent it to other outstanding Biblical scholars, in Canada and America. I realize now; I probably hoped that one of them would like it enough to get it published. That wasn't realistic; scholars aren't publishers. I hadn't published a book before and didn't know the ropes.

So it went. I decided that, in any case, Judas was too important to leave to the Biblical experts. I went back to the books, I re-read the commentaries and read the current material; I wrote and rewrote, prayed and prayed again. Judas kept appearing and re-appearing in the public mind. He has a fascination all his own, the fascination of evil, of a Hitler or a Stalin or a Bin Laden. How could Judas have done it? He was one of only 12 men whom Jesus selected to be his disciples, then apostles. 30 pieces of silver? Was Jesus, who seemed to know even what was in men's minds, that wrong about this one disciple? How could Judas identify his Lord with a kiss? Why didn't Jesus tell him to buzz off (as in *Superstar*?)

The same questions occur in the portrayals of Jesus and Judas in Andrew Lloyd Webber's *Jesus Christ Superstar* and *Godspell* and in other cinematic and literary portrayals. What was Judas playing at?

So, I finally got up my nerve and started submitting it to publishers. One evangelical publisher objected to my explanation of the Biblical rumours about the death of Judas. I pointed out that any jury or detective in the land who was given two accounts of a death which couldn't be reconciled and in the absence of a body would doubt that death had occurred (see separate section on the death of Judas). This publisher replied that he would lose what readership he had if he published my book. One of the major publishers was more encouraging, but decided in the end not to publish it. An American friend, Dr. Matthew Melko, a distinguished academic in the field of Peace Studies, offered to act as my agent and submitted it to publishers, to no avail. Dr. Matthew Melko said later, "I was surprised at the venom with which it was rejected". Judas seems to strike a raw nerve in the corporate consciousness. Back on my knees, back to the books, back to the PC, and here I am.

Judas has always had a fascination for us. Besides the aforementioned pop musicals, was he not a major character in *The Last Temptation*? Two novels about Judas (one from 1973, another from 1983) are listed in the Bibliography. More recently have appeared Jeffrey Archer's *The Gospel of Judas* and C. K. Stead's *My Name Was Judas*.

I don't believe in luck, preferring to believe we make our own luck and that God speaks directly to us when He wants us to know something. But I came close to believing in luck when my wife opened the *National Geographic* reporting the discovery of the long lost *The Gospel of Judas* just as I was getting this manuscript ready to be published. So, let's just say the Holy Spirit spoke through Peggy (see Dedication). In any case, it came at just the right time. Some of me says "50 years late" but the better part of me knows that the 50 years of prayer, study and consultation with experts in the field have produced a much stronger book. *The Gospel of Judas* strengthens the case for Judas being

Jesus' Beloved Disciple and the source of the Fourth Gospel.

I have to admit that Judas' all consuming passion has become my life long passion. It has propelled me to countless thousands of hours of study and writing over the last half century. I have come to have great admiration for Judas, Beloved Disciple, the author of the Fourth Gospel. I identify with him. My sins are mainly sins of omission while his great sin was one of commission. I fervently want his story to be known, to the glory of God.

Summation

In our Working Hypothesis (Introduction), we have moved in this great academic and spiritual adventure from postulating that the Beloved Disciple was the primary source of the Fourth Gospel. We asked the question WHY? The answer to this question made logical the quantum leap of postulating that the Beloved Disciple was Judas, who cleverly disguised his identity so that his eyewitness testimony would survive and be available to the Church. This quantum leap is presented as the best possible explanation for the appearance of a person named, *Beloved Disciple*, in the Fourth Gospel. There seems to be no better explanation. Further we postulated that the recently discovered, *The Judas Gospel*, (Chapter VIII) was an early and cruder effort, perhaps a floater, an attempt to test the water and see whether a document with name of Judas on it would reach the Christian community. Further we went on to postulate that John the disciple who, located in Ephesus, was editor to Judas' source, also contributing out of his own experience as an eyewitness. We then went on to posit that John's community, his own disciples, were also involved and served as an editorial committee, going over the Gospel, proof reading and polishing the Greek. The probable way in which this happened is presented in Chapter I. All the above is consistent with the best of ancient and modern Johannine scholarship and, in particular, dovetails neatly into R.E. Brown's five stage process. The substantiating evidence for The Working Hypothesis is first of all in the Fourth Gospel itself but there is an abundance of other substantiating evidence and this is presented in Chapters II, III, IV, V and VI.

So we have moved in our Working Hypothesis, step by step to the conclusion that Judas- Beloved Disciple was the author of the

Fourth Gospel. In this process, we have moved from possibility to probability to reasonable certainty. Anyone who questions this must be prepared to come up with a flaw in the logic and a better explanation of the facts.

In the words of the familiar hymn, Judas was *ransomed* on the cross by Jesus; *healed* of his deep inner wounds by the blood of Jesus; *restored* to the Way, the Truth and the Life by Jesus death' on the cross; *amazingly* forgiven, so wide is God's mercy, like the *wideness of the sea*.

Bibliography

The Fourth Gospel ends on this note:
"But there are also many other things which Jesus did; and were every one of them to be written, I suppose that the world itself could not contain the books that would be written." John 21.25.

This was written before the printing press, personal computers and websites. The National Geographic website is jammed by people wanting to access information on the *Gospel of Judas*. What the author of the Fourth Gospel couldn't have even imagined was the number of books which would be written about his Gospel, likewise which "the whole world can hardly contain".

Following is the tip of the iceberg. The books underlined are the ones I have found particularly useful and which are referred to in the text. The books underlined and in bold were most useful.

Allen, Willoughby C. *The Gospel According to St. Matthews* (ICC Commentary) T. & T. Clark, Edinburgh.

Appleton, George. *John's Witness to Jesus,* United Society for Christian Literature, Lutterworth Press, London, 1955.

Archer, Jeffrey, *The Gospel of Judas*

Barclay, William. *The Gospel of John*, Vol. I: ch 1-7. Revised Ed., The Saint Andrew Press, Edinburgh, 1975.

Barclay, William. *A New Testament Wordbook*, SCM Chicago, 1955.

Barclay, William. *The Master's Men,* SCM Press Ltd., Bloomsbury Street, London.

Barrett, C. K. *The Gospel According to St. John, 2nd Edition*, SPCK, London, 1978.

Bauckham, Richard. *Jesus and the Eyewitnesse,s* (Eerdmans, Grand Rapids, Michigan, 2006

Bernard, J. H. *The Gospel According to St. John* (2 vols) ICC. T. & T. Clark, Edinburgh, 1928.

Bettenson, Henry. *Documents of the Christian Church*, Oxford Univ. Press, 1954.

Brown, Raymond E. *The Community of the Beloved Disciple*, Geoffrey Chapman, London, 1979.

Brown, Raymond E. *The Gospel According to John, Vol. 29 & 29A*, Doubleday, 1966.

Bultmann, Rudolf. *The Gospel of John*, Basil Blackwell, Oxford 1971.

Cartlidge, David & David L. Duncan. *Documents for the Study of the Gospels*, William Collins, N.Y. 1980.

Childs, Brevard S. *The New Testament as Canon: An Introduction*, SCM Press, London, 1984.

Cullman, Oscar. *Peter, Disciple, Apostle, Martyr*, Translated by Floyd Filson. Living Age Books pub. by Meridian Books, Inc., New York.

Dodd, C. H. *The Interpretation of the Fourth Gospel*, Cambridge Univ. Press 1955.

Edersheim, Rev. Alfred. *The Life and Times of Jesus the Messiah* (2 vols.) Longmans, Green, and Co., New York, 1915.

Eller, Vernard. *The Beloved Disciple*, W. B. Eerdmans Publishing Co., Grand Rapids, Michigan, 1987.

Eusebius *The History of the Church*, Penguin Classics, 1965.

Goodspeed, Edgar J. *The Student's Testament,* The University of Chicago Press.

Gore, Charles (Ed). *A New Commentary on Holy Scripture*, SPCK, London 1951.

Gould, Rev. Ezra. *The Gospel According to St. Mark*, ICC, T. & T. Clark, Edinburgh.

Graves, Robert. *I, Claudius,* Arthur Bacon 1934 Publishers; also in Penguin Classics.

Harmening, William. *Forgiving Judas*

Harpur, Tom. *The Pagan Christ,* Thomas Allan, Toronto.

Harpur, Tom. *Water Into Wine,* Thomas Allan, Toronto.

Hastings, James (ed). *Dictionary of the Bible*, Rev. Ed., by Frederick C. Grant and H. H. Rowley, Charles Scribner's Sons, New York, 1963.

Hengel, Martin. *The Charismatic Leader and His Followers*, T. & T. Clark, Edinburgh, 1981.

Hengel, Martin. *The Johannine Question*, SCM London, 1989.

Hoskyns, Sir Edwyn. *The Fourth Gospel*, edited by Francis Davey (2 vols). Faber and Faber Ltd., London, 1940.

Hunter, A. M. *According to John*, SCM Press, 1968.

The Interpreter's Bible Volume VIII, New York, Abingdon Press, Nashville.

James, Montague Rhodes (translator) *The Apocryphal New Testament*, Clarendon Press, Oxford.

Jeremias, Joachim. *Unknown Sayings of Jesus*, SPCK, London, 1958.

Kanagaraj, Jey J. *'Mysticism' in the Gospel of John,* Sheffield Academic Press.

Lake, Kirsopp & F. J. Foakes (ed). *The Beginnings of Christianity*, Mcmillan & Co. London, 1920-33.

Lightfoot, R. H. *St. John's Gospel, A Commentary*. Clarendon Press, Oxford, 1956.

Lincoln, A. T. Truth on Trial; the Lawsuit Motif in the Fourth Gospel Peabody: Hendrickson, 2000.

Lincoln, A. T. the Beloved Disciple as Eyewitness and the Fourth Gospel as Witness ISNT 85 (2002).

Lindars, Barnabas. *The Gospel of John*, The New Century Bible Commentary, Marshall, Morgan & Scott, London, 1982.

Melko, Matthew. *Peace in Our Time*, Paragon House, York.

Melko, Matthew and Richard D. Weigel, *Peace in the Ancient World*, McFarland & Company, Inc., Publishers. Jefferson, N.C.

Mortenson, Greg and Relin, David Oliver. *Three Cups of Tea*, Penguin Books, 2006.

Moule, C. F. D. "The Meaning of 'Life' in the Gospels and Epistles of St. John" in Theology, A Monthly Review, March, 1975.

National Geographic Magazine, May, 2006 by Andrew Cockburn.

Novum Testamentum Graece D. Eberhard Nestle Privileg, Wurtt, Bibelanstalt, Stuttgart.

Richardson, Alan, *Theological Word Book of the Bible* The Macmillan Company.

Richardson, Cyril (ed.) *Early Christian Fathers*, The Westminster Press, Philadelphia, 1953.

Robinson, James M. *The Secrets of Judas* HarperCollins New York, N.Y., 2007

Robinson, John A. T. *Redating the New Testament*, SCM Press Ltd., London, 1976.

Robinson, John A. T. *The Priority of John*, SCM Press, 1985.

Sanders, J. N. & Charles Black, *The Gospel According to St. John*, Adam & Charles Black, London, 1968.

Scott, Ernest F. *The Fourth Gospel, Its Purpose and Theology*, 2nd ed., T. & T. Clark, Edinburgh, 1908.

Smalley, Stephen. *John – Evangelist & Interpreter*, Paternoster Press, Exxter, 1978.

Stead, C. K., *My Name was Judas*

Tasker, R. V. G. *John*, Tyndale New Testament Commentaries, Inter-Varsity Press, Leicester.

Temple, William. *Readings in St. John's Gospel*, McMillan & Co., London, 1955.

The *National Geographic* Magazine May 2006 article entitled The **Judas Gospel** ngm.com/gospel

Vanstone, W. H. *The Stature of Waiting*, Darton, Longman & Todd, London, 1982.

Westcott, B. F. *The Gospel According to St. John*, John Murray, London 1890.

Westminster Historical Atlas to the Bible, The Westminster Press, Philadelphia, 1955.

Wright, N. T. Jesus and the Victory of God (London, SPCK, 1996).

Wright, N. T. The Challenge of Jesus (London, SPCK, 2000).

In addition, two fiction books which are of great interest:

Callaghan, Morley. *A Time For Judas*, McMillan, Toronto, 1983.

Panas, Henryk. Translated from the Polish by Marc E. Heien. *The Gospel According to Judas*, Hutchinson of London, 1973.

Comments:

On a scale of succinct to encyclopediac; Barclay and Cullman are equally adept at selecting out of their immense knowledge and putting together essential information. They should not be neglected because they sometimes produce little (in size) books.

On the other end of the scale, Brown has assembled an immense amount of data to the extent that it might be thought the Johannine scholar need look no further.

But, there are others, namely two Victorian (a time of great British Biblical scholarship): British giants who are in danger of being forgotten. This would be a great loss because they have a lot to contribute.

The Gospel According to St. John by B. F. Westcott, later Bishop, 1890 This is simply the best commentary on St. John's Gospel combining insight with impeccable scholarship. I go back to it time and time again in preaching and in teaching.

The Life and Times of Jesus the Messiah by Alfred Edershem, 1915. This is a curious and very Victorian combination of scholarship and passion. He is particularly good on the classical Greek and Roman and the Jewish antecedents of the Christain religion.

I have found the American Revised Standard Version Bible to be the best modern translation into English, a worthy successor to the King James Version. Each was made by a committee, proof that God does work through committees, in spite of much evidence to the contrary. So often it seems that "a camel is a horse designed by a committee."

Charts and Illustrations

Biographical information

Bill Brison, b. 1929, 1/8 American Indian; Alfred University NY, B Sc. '51; Berkeley Divinity School, New Haven CT; M Div; STM; Deacon 1957, Priest 1957; served in two parishes in the Episcopal Church USA; Archdeacon of New Haven CT; served in three parishes in the Church of England from 1972; Archdeacon of Bolton, Manchester UK; co-author with Peggy Brison of "A Tale of Two Visits to Chechnya"; ecclesiastical distinction of being the only person made an archdeacon in these two branches of the Anglican Communion; this is mitigated by the debate among medieval theologians as to whether it is possible for an archdeacon to be admitted to heaven; thus Bill Brison is in double jeopardy relying on the wideness of God's mercy.